MW00777411

"This volume is a gem, full of concise, practical ...
information. As an attorney specializing in labor law, I
have a special appreciation of the employment related sec-
tions, which are excellent. As a business person, I found
useful information, ideas and tips on virtually every page of
every section. This book will stay in my office for regular
reference."

Robert J. Chovanec, Attorney
Warner, Norcross & Judd

"I recommend this book to clients who are starting a new
business or those wanting to make major improvements in
their business operations. Tremendous source of
information from marketing strategies to job descriptions,
from employee manuals to precision writing."

Glenn Poole, CPA
Plante & Moran

"This valuable resource provides detailed help and step-by-
step guidance for the critical issues facing today's
entrepreneurs.

Dana Locniskar, First Vice President
Merrill Lynch

"This book, read once, is interesting and informative; read
often, it becomes an invaluable executive guide; internal-
ized and implemented, its worth equates with 30 years'
experience!"

Marvin A. McCormick, President
Midstate Title Company

HIGH-IMPACT BUSINESS STRATEGIES

Everything You Need to:
Sharpen Your Competitive Edge
Increase Sales
Strengthen Your Management Practices
Help Prevent Employee Litigation
is Right Here...

by Judith A. DeLapa

© 1993 High-Impact Marketing Services
2505 East Paris Road S.E. Suite 130
Grand Rapids, Michigan 49546

© 1993 High-Impact Marketing Services.

This publication is designed to provide accurate and authoritative information in regard to the subjects covered. It is sold with the understanding that neither the author nor the publisher is engaged in rendering legal, accounting, or other professional service. If legal advice or other expert assistance is required, the services of a competent professional should be sought.

Text Design by Tamara Rix, High-Impact Marketing Services
Copy Editing by Jamie Brummel, Gina DeLapa and
Jennifer VeStrand
Cartoons by Bradford Veley, Marquette, Michigan
Cover Design by Joe Goeldel, High-Impact Marketing Services
Fulfillment by Sue Westhouse, High-Impact Marketing Services

High-Impact Marketing Services
Grand Rapids, Michigan

LIBRARY OF CONGRESS CATALOGING-IN-PUBLICATION DATA

DeLapa, Judith A.

High-impact marketing strategies : everything you need to sharpen your competitive edge, increase sales, strengthen your management practices, help prevent employee litigation / by Judith A. DeLapa

Library of Congress Catalog Card Number: 93-80028

ISBN 0-9638432-0-6

$19.95 Softcover

Printed in the United States of America

*Dedicated to
James P. DeLapa, my husband,
mentor and confidant.*

How to order:

Quantity discounts are available by calling toll-free 1-800-444-2524 or fax your request on your letterhead, include information concerning the intended use of the books and the number of the books you wish to purchase, to (813) 753-9396.

TABLE OF CONTENTS

CHAPTER 1
SHARPEN YOUR COMPETITIVE EDGE:
DEVELOP A FORMAL BUSINESS PLAN

CHAPTER 2
MASTER LEAD GENERATION AND YOU
WILL NEVER RUN OUT OF QUALIFIED
PROSPECTS

CHAPTER 3
AUTOMATE THE SALES PROCESS AND
WATCH SALES SOAR!

CHAPTER 4
MANAGING THE SALES PROCESS: THE
SECRET TO INCREASING SALES

CHAPTER 5
HOW TO WRITE BUSINESS
PROPOSALS LIKE A PRO

CHAPTER 6
JOB DESCRIPTIONS THAT
REALLY WORK

CHAPTER 7
HOW TO CONDUCT EFFECTIVE
PERFORMANCE APPRAISALS

CHAPTER 8
HOW TO WRITE OR UPDATE YOUR
EMPLOYEE MANUAL

CHAPTER 9
NOW YOU CAN WRITE MORE DYNAMIC REPORTS AND MEMOS

CHAPTER 10
PRECISION WRITING MADE EASY

CHAPTER 11
HOW TO CONDUCT A CUSTOMER SURVEY AND ADDRESS QUALITY ISSUES HEAD-ON

CHAPTER 12
PREPARING YOUR COMPANY'S FIRST
ANNUAL REPORT

FINAL THOUGHTS

ACKNOWLEDGMENTS

To our clients and customers who have made this book possible. This book is a compilation of what we have learned together. The challenges they have given us and the confidence they placed in us have enabled us to expand our horizons, go beyond our comfort zone and accomplish remarkable things.

To Gina DeLapa and Tom Owen for their inspiration and guidance in the creation and editing of the original manuscripts.

To Jennifer VeStrand for her patience in editing and proofing the manuscript.

To Jamie Brummel for editing and compiling the manuscript.

To Tamara J. Rix for her creativity and attention to detail in designing the inside of the book.

To Joe Goeldel for his talent in designing the front and back covers.

ABOUT THE AUTHOR

The author, a graduate of Michigan State University with B.S. and M.A. degrees, has been the co-owner of one business and founder/sole proprietor of two others.

In 1963 she co-founded a business with her husband, Jim, in a converted garage, and 13 years later Saluto Foods Corporation, conducting business in 27 states and with more than 250 employees, was sold to a Fortune 100 company.

Today, Judy is CEO of High-Impact Marketing Services, which she founded in 1987. In 1989 she was recognized by *Human Resource Executive* for developing one of the "top 20 human resource products of the year," an easy-to-customize Employee Personnel Manual on computer disk, now available in three editions: General Business, Foodservice and Healthcare.

Judy is an active member of the Grand Rapids Area Chamber of Commerce where she served as CEO Roundtable leader and was selected to participate in the year-long program, Leadership Grand Rapids. She is actively involved in community service work.

She serves on the Advisory Board of The National Bureau of Professional Management Consultants, the Advisory Board of Ad Response MicroMarketing Corporation and has provided assessment, consulting and marketing services for a wide variety of service and manufacturing businesses. Judy's area of specialization is researching, developing and implementing key business strategies to increase the effectiveness and profitability of small- and medium-size businesses.

CHAPTER 1

SHARPEN YOUR COMPETITIVE EDGE: DEVELOP A FORMAL BUSINESS PLAN

For every entrepreneur who made it without strategic planning or who didn't develop a formal business plan until he or she needed outside capital, hundreds have failed for lack of direction.

We live in an era of constant change. Demographic, economic and global changes are bombarding us faster than we can comprehend and assimilate what it all means. That is why a formal business plan and strategic planning are vital to your business's survival and success.

There is no absolute one-and-only way to develop a formal business plan. But accountants, bankers and other professionals who may review your plan will evaluate your business's potential for success and make decisions based on your plan's content and the way you present it. Therefore, your business plan must be well-conceived and executed so it represents you and your business accurately.

This chapter will show you how to develop both a strategic plan and a formal business plan that will serve your needs and command the respect of those who read them. Many areas in the strategic plan and the business plan overlap. The topics are presented separately here, however, so that you can implement either plan independently of the other. A business plan is a more formal document that includes financial projections and has several years' longevity. A strategic plan is an action plan that you redevelop each year.

Developing Your Formal Business Plan

The development of your business plan will require time and commitment from you and your key people. The time and effort you spend developing and fine-tuning your plan will pay dividends, however, not only for the coming year, but for the life of your business.

Benefits of Having a Formal Business Plan

A formal business plan:

- Serves as a valuable management tool

- Provides potential investors and lenders with the information they need to make financial decisions

- Focuses the energy of your business in a single, forward direction

- Provides a benchmark against which to compare actual income and expenses with projections and budgets

- Forces your management team to integrate diverse ideas and resolve potential conflicts before they happen.

Getting Started

Getting started may be the hardest part, but remember that your plan will be revised many times before it is completed. Even though business plans are usually presented in the sequence listed below, you may actually develop the plan in any order you wish.

- Executive summary

- Company profile
- Products/Services
- Marketing/Sales
- Organization charts
- Key personnel
- Financial projections
- Primary goals for current year
- Optional attachments

One way to begin is to record, on tape or in writing, information about your business from your key people. Have the information typed and distributed before your first meeting; this can serve as a draft and a springboard to the next level. Use the most current version of the plan as a basis for moving forward with each subsequent meeting. Revisions and refinements will continue until the plan is finished. Don't delay implementation of the plan until it's perfect. The value of your plan is only as great as the action that follows. Set a target date for completion, schedule a series of meetings, make the completion of your business plan a priority and it will get done.

The development process requires:

- Analytical problem solving
- Examining options
- Questioning existing and new assumptions
- Assessing opportunities
- Determining resources you'll need to meet your projections
- Setting priorities.

The development process may not be smooth. But your persistence will pay off as you channel the thinking of the team and focus the energy of the business in a single direction.

After your management team has developed the business plan and before it is finalized, communicate the plan to other workers for their input and to gain the widespread buy-in and commitment you'll need to ensure its success. Communicating the plan will:

- Help your key people internalize and further commit to the plan as they "sell" it to others

- Clearly identify for everyone the direction your management team has charted and the strategies you'll use to get there

- Demonstrate to everyone that you need and value their support to make the plan a reality.

How to Develop Each Part of Your Formal Business Plan

Executive Summary

The executive summary provides a quick overview of the entire plan. Its purpose is to give the reader enough background information about your business to make the rest of your report meaningful. Write the mission statement early in the process of formulating your business plan, but write the rest of the executive summary last.

Your mission statement should answer these questions:

- What is the purpose of the business?

- Whom do we serve?

- What is our primary goal?

In addition to your mission statement, the executive summary should include:

- A brief description of your product(s) or service(s)

- A brief description of your marketing strategy

- A statement of your revenue projections

- A statement describing your business structure

- A thumbnail sketch of your management team.

Company Profile

- *Structure of your business*—Is it a corporation, sub-S, proprietorship or partnership? Has it always been the same? If not, note the years changes occurred.

- *Location*—Describe the location and number of square feet in your facility.

- *Years in business*—Summarize major events, new product introductions or stages of growth if yours is an established business.

- *Workers*—List the number of workers and a percentage or numerical breakdown of management, administrative, sales and production workers.

- *Distribution*—Explain how customers obtain your products or services.

Products/Services

- Current line of products and/or services

- Frequency with which your company introduces new products or services

- Product/service mix by percent of sales as it is today and as you would like it to be

- How your products or services meet customer needs.

Marketing/Sales

- Demographic description of target customers

- Your competitive edge

- Your market share and marketing reach as it relates to the potential size of the market

- Industry trends as they relate to your business

- Marketing strategies and techniques you employ

- Strength and effectiveness of your sales team.

Organization Charts

- As your company is today

- As your company will need to be to meet your 1-year goals (may or may not be the same as your company is today)

- As your company's organization must be to meet your 3- or 5-year goals.

Key Personnel

- Describe the educational background, relevant experience, length of service and special strengths of key employees.

- Explain your organizational development plans, including training, internships, mentor-relationships and staffing projections to correspond to your financial projections. You may also want to include actual job descriptions of key employees.

Financial Projections

You and your management team should anticipate questions the reader might ask and provide full information. Enlist the help of your accountant or CPA in developing this portion of the plan, which should include:

- Equity financing you will provide
- Debt and equity financing you will need from other sources
- Sales projections (1-year and either 3- or 5-year)
- Pro forma (1-year and 3- or 5-year)—match to sales projections
- Cash-flow projections
- Break-even analysis
- Capital expenditures budget
- Assumptions used in preparing projections.

This presentation of your business plan will be greatly enhanced by colorful, well-designed graphs to illustrate your projections more dramatically.

Primary Goals for Current Year

List your primary goals for the current year to communicate your priorities and to show that your plan is realistic and attainable.

Optional Attachments

- Patents, contracts or letters of intent
- Awards, favorable publicity or other recognition
- Marketing pieces, logo or other significant information that may affect your growth and/or success.

Attach the above only if they lend needed support or credibility to other portions of the plan. Communicate your reasons for including each one, unless the reasons are obvious.

Packaging Your Formal Business Plan

Once you and your key people have finished developing your formal business plan and have communicated it to your entire team, pass it on to a competent staff member or outside service to edit and format on desktop publishing. Develop a Table of Contents and a front and back cover.

You'll want your final presentation to be professional and flawless. Once you've proofread and given final approval to the plan, have it copied on high-quality paper with heavier stock for the covers and an appropriate binding. You'll then have a plan you'll be proud to hand your bankers or other professionals who have reason to review it. Have extra copies made to fill unexpected needs.

Developing Your Strategic Plan

What Is Strategic Planning?

Strategic planning is the process of analyzing, planning and evaluating business strategies believed to be critical to helping the company achieve its goals and projections.

Successful strategic plans must be supported from the top but developed by those responsible for making them happen. Most plans become written documents; the real value of the plan, however, lies in the thinking that goes into its development and the effort that goes into its successful implementation.

Strategies are not to be confused with tactics. Strategies are action plans. Tactics are individual actions within the plan. For example: A company may decide to launch a new product. Their strategy is to market it through a series of print ads in various media. A single ad in their industry trade journal would be one tactic within their overall strategy.

How to Develop Your Strategic Plan

During the planning process, consult key people in your organization. Encourage and expect participants to think and even openly disagree. They should question each other's assumptions, identify the company's strengths and weaknesses—as well as their competitors'—and set realistic goals for themselves. Drafting the strategic plan will force the group to integrate diverse ideas and resolve conflicts that might not have been resolved any other way.

You may use various methods and techniques when developing your strategic plan. Following is a list of appropriate steps for management in small- to medium-sized businesses:

- Analyze the business as it is today

- Develop or re-evaluate your mission statement.

- Establish goals

- Define your marketing strategy

- Develop a promotional strategy

- Determine your product mix

- Develop a pricing strategy

- Develop a distribution strategy

- Determine the impact of the plan on your business.

Analyzing the Business as It Is Today

Begin by developing a one-page description of your business. Include the following:

- The date the business was established

- Its structure (sole proprietorship, partnership, corporation, sub-S)

- Its strengths and weaknesses

- Your broad goals

- What makes your business unique

- Your own competitive advantage

- List of the most critical issues to be addressed in the plan.

Developing or Re-evaluating Your Mission Statement

Your mission statement can be a condensation of the business description and should answer these questions:

- What is the purpose of our business?

- Whom do we serve?

- What is our primary goal?

It is this mission that guides you in developing your marketing strategies, goals and operational and financial strategies.

Establishing Goals

Set goals for each critical issue identified in the business analysis. Each goal should state what is to be accomplished, the time frame, and quantity or quality standards to be achieved. Limit this section to your six to eight most important goals. For example: To increase productivity in the plant by 22% within six months with no increase in rework.

Or: To increase sales by 15% per month over last year, beginning January 1, with no increase in the sales force or promotional allowances.

Defining Your Marketing Strategy

In this section, you will outline how you will carry out the strategic plan. First, analyze and define your market. Narrow your description to the segment of the market you want and the specific niche you are targeting. Identify your competition by name. List your own competitive advantages. Which segments of your market hold the greatest opportunities? What is the potential for growth?

Establish a profile of your customers, being as specific as possible. If you market to other businesses, what kinds of industries are they from? How many employees do they have? What are their sales volumes? Are they sophisticated and enlightened, or are they operating with yesterday's technology—or no technology at all?

If your customers are consumers, what are their incomes? Where do they live? What are their occupations? What are their ages?

Does your market area contain more potential customers that match this profile? How did you attract the top 25% of your customers? Your top 50%? How are the top 50% of your customers different from the bottom 50%? How can you reach more customers like the top 50%? Can you afford to continue doing business with the bottom 25%?

What needs and wants does your product or service fulfill for your customers? How do you maintain customers' interest and loyalty? What else would they buy from you that you could provide at a profit? How will your company react and adjust to changes in the market?

Describe your competitors. How well do you stack up against them? What advantages and disadvantages will you have in competing with them? Are you vying for the same customers? What can you do to gain a stronger competitive edge for the market niche you've selected?

Developing a Promotional Strategy

How will you let your customers and prospects know about your goods and services? How did you attract those who are now your best customers? What gaps in your promotional strategy or sales process are costing you customers or lost opportunity sales to existing customers?

Will your strategy enable you to achieve the desired level of sales across your marketing mix? Is the strategy affordable? How will you measure results?

Promotional strategies vary from business to business and will be affected by your market niche and your customers' motivations. But in nearly every business, a combination of several tactics will be more effective than any single approach. Weigh and consider the costs, benefits and reach of the following in developing your promotional strategies:

- Direct-mail campaigns

- Yellow Pages ads

- Brochures

- Telemarketing

- Promotional newsletter

- Professional/civic organizations

- Directory listings

- Networking/social activities

- Newspaper advertisements

- Annual open house
- Promotional offers
- Trade journal/magazine ads.

Determining Your Product Mix

Your product mix is an integral part of your marketing and promotional strategies. When establishing your product mix, ask yourself these five questions:

- Are we taking advantage of all the sales opportunities within this marketing niche, given the products and services we have to offer?

- Are there logical product/service extensions we could add to better serve our customers and enhance profits?

- Which of our products/services are most profitable when all costs are considered?

- Which product/service offerings will help us gain the most new customers per marketing dollar spent?

- Which product/service offerings are absorbing our resources and preventing us from expanding more lucrative areas of our business?

Now that you've performed your market analysis and identified your market niche, you're ready to develop your marketing strategy. Summarize your marketing strategy in a single paragraph that describes your product and service mix, pricing policy and how you will communicate with your target market. Focus on clear-cut strategies for reaching your goals. This analysis should illuminate new opportunities. Conversely, it may reveal that certain product lines and customers need to be abandoned in order to expand your business in more profitable directions. Decisions to explore new opportunities and abandon unprofitable product/service lines should be made rationally rather than emotionally and implemented in an orderly transition.

Developing a Pricing Strategy

Your pricing strategy is a vital part of your strategic plan. Remember: Not every product needs to be offered at the same markup; rather, overall margins on your established product mix must be sufficient for you to operate at your projected profit level. When establishing a pricing strategy, consider the following:

- Costs (including production, marketing, inventory and delivery)

- Economic conditions

- Perceived value by customers

- Availability of identical goods/services from other sources

- Competitors' prices

- Value-added benefits your company provides or makes available

- Risk (Are you building in a sufficient margin to provide the quality required to ensure customer satisfaction and the level of service customers expect?)

If your pricing strategy includes written agreements or contracts, draft an original document yourself that contains all the information you need to include. Then take the draft to your attorney to rewrite it in correct legal language. Encourage your attorney to make the contract fair to both sides and as non-threatening and customer-friendly as possible. Have your attorney provide the contract to you in hard copy and on computer disk so you can use selected paragraphs and add, delete and modify each contract as necessary to meet the specific needs of each customer.

Developing a Distribution Strategy

What method of distribution will be most cost-effective for you while ensuring on-time delivery to your customers? What options can you offer customers? Will your methods meet or exceed customer expectations for quality, convenience and service?

Determining the Impact on Your Business

The last step in developing your strategic plan is to review your newly defined mission, goals and strategies and to assess the demands they will place on your business.

- Is the total plan, as it now stands, affordable?

- What new equipment will you need to support the plan?

- Do you have the necessary space and an adequate facility to carry out the plan?

- Do you have the human resources to support the plan?

- Does your business have the leadership and the key players to implement the plan?

- Are you willing and able to commit the additional resources necessary to make the plan a reality?

Implementing Your Plans

The biggest mistake you can make after developing your formal business plan and your strategic plan is to put them on the shelf and forget about them. These are

"After painstaking analysis, we can confidently predict that consumers will continue to buy scads of the goofiest things imaginable, from a bunch of companies none of us have ever heard of. That's about as far as we got!"

working documents. Every goal you set, every new product you introduce, every promotion you run, every key employee you hire, every major decision must be evaluated as it relates to your strategic plan. If it doesn't fit, it doesn't belong.

Now that you have a formal business plan and a strategic plan, revamp your income statements to show monthly and year-to-date figures, and compare actual figures with projections by a plus (+) or minus (-) deviation. An important function of your overall plan is to highlight the need for corrective action early while there's still time to intervene and make a difference.

Keep in mind: A plan is just a plan. That's all it is. Plans aren't reality, and plans don't always work out as expected. That doesn't mean the plan isn't good or that it doesn't have value or that the time spent developing the plan was wasted.

The real value of the plan is its function as a guide and a benchmark. Properly used, a good plan will make crystal clear what needs to be done and point to the specific areas where corrective action needs to be taken.

Planning—forecasting—budgeting—tracking—evaluating—correcting. It's a continuous cycle that ensures your success.

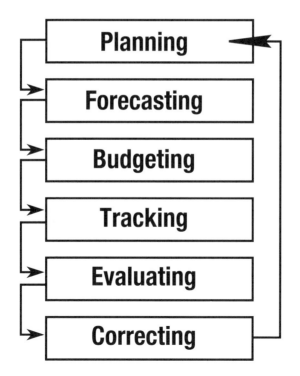

Deciding What to Do if the Plans Don't Work

More people make the mistake of staying in business too long than getting out too soon. If your business isn't making it, enlist the help of your management team to determine why not and what strategies and opportunities you may have overlooked. Even though you've done some of this already, do it again. You've invested too much time, effort and resources not to go back to the drawing board for another assessment and evaluation to determine what went wrong.

First, analyze the problem(s); have you taken the right steps to correct them? Is the problem a lack of sales? Are your prices too high? too low? Is there a market for your product or service? Are certain expenses out of line? How about marketing/advertising—is it working? Are marketing or advertising expenses too high?

Is your cost of sales too high? How about waste and returns? Where can you cut expenses? Are there individuals, departments or divisions that are pulling down the rest of your operation?

After you have identified the problems and possible solutions, analyze the potential consequences of your solutions. What else can you do? Put your thoughts down on paper. List what's working—what's not. Spend some quality time with professionals outside the business who can study the situation objectively: a business consultant, your accountant or someone else whose business acumen you respect. With their help and your own best effort determine if the problem(s) can be remedied. How long will it take? Can you afford to stay with it? If you succeed at turning the business around, will the payoff be worth the effort and risk?

By analyzing the problems in this manner, you'll discover your own answers. If the ship is sinking, why stay with it? Cut your losses. There will be other opportunities. But don't be too quick to react. Take some time to reflect on where you've been and how you got there before seeking other opportunities.

Operating a successful business today requires a very disciplined approach as well as a superior product or service that can be strategically marketed at a competitive price. But even that is not enough. You must also have the staying power, a team of competent people and the ability to provide the leadership required to pull it all together.

Operating a successful business is a daily challenge and an exhilarating experience. Not everyone is cut out for this lifestyle; others can't imagine life being any other way. The important thing is deciding what's best for you.

CHAPTER 2

MASTER LEAD GENERATION AND YOU WILL NEVER RUN OUT OF QUALIFIED PROSPECTS

Many executives, managers and business owners put into practice an old saying: "You can't bank on yesterday's news." In today's rapidly changing global marketplace, these same individuals are realizing that you can't bank on yesterday's business or, more importantly, yesterday's customers. It is crucial for businesses to implement a systematic approach to generating new customers and cultivating long-term client relationships. It is even more important to continually cultivate and seek ways to better serve the customers you already have.

Lead generation and lead qualification: two of the hottest buzz words in today's marketplace. Sales lead generation can be defined as activity that identifies potential customers and sales. Sales lead qualification identifies the importance and value of each new sales lead. Unfortunately, too many companies and businesses fail to recognize the importance of lead generation and lead qualification until it's too late.

Companies and organizations need to constantly develop new opportunities for selling their products and services if they are to grow. It is difficult to sustain a viable organization if your company's performance is directly tied to the performance of a limited target group. A flow of new business opportunities into your organization will allow you to differentiate your product and service offerings and to meet the needs of an expanding audience. This will enable you to maximize the returns from your products, services and available resources.

Lead generation and qualification will provide many benefits to your company or organization. These benefits include increased:

- *Effectiveness*—A well-defined lead generation program will produce the maximum number of new leads for the marketing dollars you spend. A systematic approach to lead qualification will help ensure that all action steps within the sales process are focused on generating additional sales dollars.

- *Efficiency*—Effective lead generation and qualification will help ensure that your sales team spends more time on actual selling activities. This will reduce the overall cost of each sale and generate sales more quickly.

- *Profitability*—Lead generation and qualification enables you to sell your products and services to a broader audience, thus allowing you to practice system selling. System selling will help you combine products and services to achieve higher overall margins per sale. In addition, effective lead generation/ qualification will help maximize the impact of your advertising and promotional activities.

In this chapter we'll look at various lead sources available to you as well as several methods you can use to generate new leads. Then we'll walk you through a systematic approach for lead qualification and provide guidelines for implementing a sound lead generation/ qualification program in your business or organization.

Lead Generation

Many people practice lead generation activities every day and don't even realize it. Just reading the newspaper or your favorite trade journal or business magazine produces names of companies and individuals you may consider likely candidates for your product or service. In everyday conversations with acquaintances and other business people, potential sales opportunities pop up frequently.

Let's focus on two significant areas of lead generation: lead sources and generation methods.

Lead Sources

There are three primary sources for leads:

- People within your company or organization
- Public sources
- Purchased lists and files.

Leads Within Your Company or Organization

Internal lead sources may be the easiest and least expensive to get. These can include any files you may have on past clients and customers or records from past promotional and advertising campaigns. To be useful, the information must still be accurate.

Communicate the importance of lead generation to all those within your organization. You will be surprised at the number of references and referrals you can get from your own employees or co-workers, especially your sales staff. Have your sales staff identify the type of company that represents your customers. Also, have them develop criteria and characteristics that identify your best potential customers. This is called your customer profile.

Another good source of leads is companies or organizations with whom you work closely. Maintain good relations with your vendors; share sales and customer lead information. Companies with whom you have a strong working relationship will provide mutual benefits and leads that result in sales.

Leads From Public Sources

There are numerous public resources you can use to generate leads, including city directories, phone directories or Yellow Pages. Considering that the average sales call costs $240 or more, it really is wise to "let your fingers do the walking."

Another great resource for effective leads is the public library. Select from specialized business directories, such as the *Thomas Register,* newspapers from all major cities, virtually every magazine in print, and major trade publications. All of these sources can be used to generate specific, targeted potential sales for your business.

Leads From Purchased Lists and Files

The third lead source is a rented or purchased list of semi-qualified data. These lists can be obtained from list brokers or publishers of trade journals or compiled from directories you purchase. Many of these lists can be highly targeted depending on the demographic specifications you establish. Most lists are available in your choice of formats including hard copy, mailing labels, magnetic tape and personal computer diskettes.

List rental has become a very big and sophisticated business where the caution "Let the buyer beware" applies. Always test the list before committing to large quantities. (Most lists have a 5,000 name minimum, but you can always test 1,000 or 2,500 before spending the postage for the entire 5,000.)

Lead Generation Methods

Once you have determined how you are going to get leads, you have many methods available to you to generate sales and customer leads. Whatever method you choose to implement, the objective is to reach the audience that wants and needs your products and services. You must measure the results of your lead generation activity so you know which method(s) works best for you. The greater the value of an average customer, the more you'll be able to spend to generate one new customer. For example: The company selling cars can afford to spend more money to generate a new customer than can the company operating a car wash.

"And this is our Marketing Department. They've been going through some major downsizing lately."

Advertising

Advertising is designed to create broad awareness and interest in your company, products and services. Effective advertising campaigns normally incorporate response mechanisms with a call to action. The response mechanism can be in the form of a toll-free 800 number. Some companies are now passing on the cost of product or service information to customers by listing a 900 number, which is a chargeable call. Other response mechanisms include reader response cards, such as those found in trade journals. These response cards are sent to the publisher who then provides a printout of names, addresses and telephone numbers to each company whose ads brought inquiries.

Another popular type of advertisement is reader card decks, a package of coupons or advertisements on 3"x5" cards to be returned directly to the company whose products are featured on the card.

Promotions

Product and service promotions are another important lead generation method. These are very targeted campaigns designed for a specific action. Normally, promotions are designed to draw a large number of leads in a very short period of time. Promotions can be used to introduce new products, to announce sales and special offers, and to promote after-sale services.

Special Events

Special events, such as open houses and seminars on the products and services you market, are another effective lead generation tool. These events are usually informative and focus on the value of your products and services as a solution to your customers' problems or specific needs. Special events are an excellent way to meet potential customers and build customer confidence in your products and services.

Direct Marketing

Direct marketing is one of the most effective ways to generate leads. Direct marketing communicates your specific marketing message directly to your target audience. The two most basic forms of direct marketing include direct mail and telemarketing.

Direct Mail

Almost every adult has experienced some form of direct mail contact. Can you honestly say you've never been tempted by million-dollar sweepstakes or offers to join book or tape clubs? This form of mass mailing is designed to generate immediate response. The call to action is usually within 30 days, and the tactic is designed to produce a high number of leads to generate many smaller-volume sales transactions. This type of mailing usually focuses on consumer sales. Catalog merchandising is a longer-term method of direct, consumer-oriented mail solicitation.

A more frequent tactic for business-to-business marketing is a targeted direct mail program. This type of program is designed to produce long-term clients rather than short-term sales. Depending on the product or service being marketed, there may be a lower number of initial leads but a higher frequency of contacts, which could result in a higher percentage of sales per lead. This tactic often involves a series of contacts with your target audience. These could be letters or other printed materials sent out at very short intervals, possibly seven to ten days apart, designed to generate a response from individual prospects.

Other types of targeted mailing programs include newsletters. Newsletters target customers and prospects so that the organization's name and marketing message are communicated on a regular basis. While some companies use newsletters that focus on their own particular industry, other companies prefer alternative newsletters that appeal to a broader audience and readership. These newsletters achieve their objective by offering significant take-away value for the reader. Newsletters that are totally self-serving most often end up in the "round file." Thus, the sender's objective of making an impact on the target audience is lost unless he or she is willing to provide useful information to readers and potential customers.

Telemarketing

Most business owners either love or hate telemarketing. There's no in-between. Telemarketing is normally used to sell products with short sales cycles such as non-technical, consumer-oriented products. But telemarketing for business-to-business marketing can be very effective in supplementing media, print or direct marketing activities by further qualifying the lead.

Telemarketing is becoming one of the most effective methods for initial personal contact between buyer and seller. This initial contact is important because it sets the stage for the rest of the sales process. For a telemarketing program to be effective, it is extremely important that it be a planned activity, staffed by skilled professionals who are knowledgeable about the product and services, and that the marketing message be scripted. This script must facilitate the question-and-answer process that takes place over the phone and build confidence in both parties.

Your telemarketing activities should be designed to increase the efficiency of your overall sales process. Telemarketing supplements the direct sales call, and it can facilitate your customer service activities.

The most effective method of direct marketing, however, is a combination of direct mail and telemarketing to produce a high percentage of responses. A series of letters combined with professional, courteous telemarketing can create awareness and excitement about your products and services. The power of catalogs, television and credit cards has fostered a new market for immediate sales capitalizing on customers willing to make spontaneous purchases.

Lead Qualification

Many businesses measure the effectiveness of their lead generation campaign by the number of leads generated. But actually, the most important aspect of any lead generation program is the quality of the lead generated. The only way to measure the quality of the lead is to implement a systematic lead qualification process, which ultimately tracks the sales resulting from the leads.

We defined lead qualification as processes that identify the importance and value of each new customer or sales lead. Assigning a value to each potential new customer separates the leads into categories that can be effectively managed. These categories classify each lead as a hot lead, a viable prospect, a lead of long-term importance, or a lead that is unlikely to buy products or services. This rating system will help you establish a time frame for prospect development and allocate resources as you develop each new sales lead.

There are three steps to the lead qualification process:

- Identify and document the sales cycle for your products and services.

- Develop a customer profile for all your leads and customers.

- Establish a target list of potential customers and sales.

The Sales Cycle

Every product or service offering has a sales cycle. This cycle can be defined as the major steps involved in bringing the process to sale. Each step, sometimes referred to as a plateau or a milestone, requires a specific set of marketing and sales actions.

Many products and services require action steps similar to these:

- Scheduling an appointment

- Making an initial visit

- Leaving a brochure or other literature

- Making a presentation

- Reviewing pricing

- Preparing a proposal

- Presenting the proposal and price quotation

- Closing the sale.

Other products and services require specific action steps to complete the sales process. Products and services that are technical in nature or that require capital expenditures may be complex and involve numerous contacts over a long period of time. Action steps in these processes may include such things as:

- Performing a needs assessment
- Reviewing findings and perceptions with the client
- Demonstrating the product
- Conducting factory or on-site visits
- Completing design specifications
- Sending design templates
- Installing a mock-up
- Presenting the cost justification
- Submitting the bid proposal.

Make each step of the sales cycle measurable. This will help you determine time frame goals for each new sales and customer lead, allowing you to accurately forecast the sale. Then track the activity and the time required for each step of every lead.

Customer Profiles

A customer profile is nothing more than a blueprint of information for that specific customer. Each blueprint should contain answers to a series of questions that address four primary issues for every sales and customer lead you generate.

Issue 1: Authority

Your lead profile should contain validated information relative to a person's decision-making power for your products and services. Start your investigation high within that company's organizational structure to determine who you need to target. You can always move down to a lower level easier than you can move up the corporate ladder. It may be helpful to understand the management philosophy of the customer or lead to help you determine the level at which decisions are made rel-

ative to your products and services. For instance, a
decentralized management philosophy usually
allows decisions to be made closer to the problem or
opportunity.

Issue 2: Requirements

Capture information about the lead that will tell you
why they need to buy your products and services:

- What are their short-term and long-term needs?

- What applications will your products and services be
  expected to meet?

- What is this lead's sales cycle?

- What are the competitive products that are currently
  being used or considered?

- What competitors will you be up against?

- Are the competitors in a more or less advantageous
  position to service future customer needs?

It may be helpful to determine whether your products or services are being purchased as an expense item
or a capital item. The latter normally requires a higher
level and longer term of decision-making.

Issue 3: Budget

The lead profile should identify the amount of
money budgeted for your products and services and how
often the customer needs to buy this product. Translate
the lead's interest into quantifiable terms so that you can
estimate a budget if your lead is not willing to disclose
that information. Will you be likely to benefit from
future business if you capture the initial order?

Issue 4: Time Frame

Assign all sales and customer leads specific steps within your sales cycle so that you can get a better understanding of the aggregate demand upon your available resources. This will then allow you to set priorities according to which leads are most important and which may require special resources.

Target Lists

Define your overall customer and sales lead lists according to the target market you established within your sales plan. This market offers you the highest potential for increasing your sales and market share and is the area where you will focus your sales effort and other resources. It is the market that best fits your product mix and thus will give you the greatest return.

Your sales staff is an excellent resource for helping you accurately define your total available target market. Structure your lists according to the types of industry within your target market or the type of products and services you will be selling to specific customers. Place every lead you generate into this list initially as a starting block for further prospect development activities.

Lead generation and qualification can be as easy as opening up the Yellow Pages, making a phone call and asking a series of questions. The objective is to develop qualified leads that you can further prospect toward a sale.

Effective Lead Generation and Qualification Implementation

Establish Goals and Objectives

Goals and objectives must be measurable in order for you to analyze the performance of any action your company takes. But lead generation may involve certain intangible characteristics that go beyond easy-to-measure characteristics.

Take into account the following when establishing your lead generation goals and objectives:

- *Quality vs. Quantity*—The objective of most advertising and promotional programs is to generate leads. But the objective of your sales force should be to focus on high-quality sales leads that offer the greatest potential for sales.

- *Customers vs. Clients*—Customers provide your organization with short-term sales transactions. Clients are customers with whom you have developed a long-term relationship, thereby increasing the opportunity for maintaining sales volumes. You must determine the optimum balance of customers and clients in order to maximize your sales and marketing resources.

- *Sales Objectives vs. Budgets*—Together, your sales objectives and your budget will determine how aggressively you can generate and qualify new leads. Work to maximize the return on each dollar invested toward generating new business.

Developing a Database

The database is a summary of all the customer profile information you have collected on prospects, customers and clients. The customer profiles not only ensure the database remains consistent from one name to the other, but they also allow you to retrieve only the data you need to address certain issues, problems or opportunities your sales force may be experiencing.

Structure the database so it is easy to use and allows information to flow smoothly in and out of your sales organization. The database contains knowledge about your prospects and customers. Knowledge builds confidence, and confidence will help your sales force make informed decisions and bring about quick and effective sales.

Your database can be effectively utilized if it is structured centrally within the organization. This will add integrity, consistency and accuracy to your data, thus increasing the value of your database.

Your database is a valuable asset to your company, and a centrally located database must be protected. This can be accomplished by establishing a set of procedures that will govern the use and maintenance of your database. Consider assigning one person to be your database administrator and oversee all activities involving the database. This person is also responsible for developing and enforcing procedures that everyone must follow when using the database.

It may be necessary to develop marketing tools that will ensure these procedures are followed. These tools can include:

• Sales lead forms

• Telemarketing scripts and questionnaires

• Sales call reports

- Prospect and customer surveys

- Customized management reports.

Make sure your database is protected and secure. Certain documents should be duplicated and stored in a protected area off premises and possibly in an area that is also fireproof. It is wise to keep some information, such as financial information and customer transactions, for as long as 5 to 7 years. Periodically, however, purge your database of old or inactive accounts with whom you no longer conduct business.

Integrating Your Database With Your Sales Process

Design your database so your customer profiles can be segmented as follows:

- *Rating*—Assign all prospects and customers a rating of importance. Make the rating simple, such as A, B, C or 1, 2, 3, as described on page 43.

- *Demographics*—Demographic information on each of your prospects and customers is important in order to perform effective target marketing techniques. This will allow you to maximize your available resources in generating leads within your target market.

- *Product and service mix*—It is important to know who your customers are for which products and services. This will allow you to determine and forecast demand for any one product or service and help you further target that product or service to the right audience.

The key strategy is to make every sales and marketing activity an action step within your sales process. This helps to ensure that you turn your prospect or lead into a sale as quickly as possible and that you continue to build a long-term selling relationship with that client.

It is equally important to establish a strategy that allows you to track each lead through the sales process. Every activity within an action step should be documented for each lead and customer in order to measure the performance of that action. This allows you to establish benchmarks for your sales process. Performance improvement strategies can then be implemented to increase the profitability of your organization.

Keys to Implementing an Effective Lead Generation/Qualification Process

Effective lead generation helps you manage a successful sales and marketing process. The objectives are to generate more leads, quickly develop leads into sales, and establish higher value, longer-term relationships with certain clients. These activities will result in an improved sales process, including higher return for your advertising and promotional dollars. You'll spend less time cultivating a lead into a sale, which in turn will yield higher profit margins.

There are a wealth of sources available from which to generate leads. The combination of methods used to implement lead generation can be endless; however, it is an established fact that the most effective method for generating and qualifying leads is a combination of advertising, direct mail and telemarketing.

Lead qualification is the process that differentiates your leads into identifiable opportunities for your company. It is important that the sales cycle for your products and services accommodate each specific lead

according to its profile. Remember the four questions
that need to be resolved: authority, requirement, budget
and time frame.

Align your lead generation goals and objectives with
those of your strategic plan. Develop and maintain an
accurate, up-to-date database that can become the foundation of your overall sales process, and implement
strategies that maximize your available resources.
Determine if quantity or quality is the most important
factor in your lead generation process. Make all of your
activities action steps, and make them count.

Your time in front of your customer is limited.
Accurate information is necessary for each lead, customer, and client to make an informed decision.
Informed decisions increase your chances of getting the
sale and improve each step of your sales process. These
are the keys to implementing an effective lead generation
and qualification process.

CHAPTER 3

AUTOMATE THE SALES PROCESS AND WATCH SALES SOAR!

Sales are the driving force behind most successful companies. And a company's lifeline is its customers. But today's global marketplace is becoming much more competitive, and customers have more alternatives than ever when it comes to purchasing the goods and services they want.

Information is at the heart of this trend. We live, market and sell in an information-oriented society. Rarely do we make a purchase without inadvertently revealing additional demographic information about ourselves. Examples of this are everywhere:

- Purchasing groceries with your new bank card that records time, transaction and amount, then ties it in to all other data stored in the bank's information pool.

- Renewing a subscription to your favorite trade journal and completing a survey that identifies your authority to make the purchase, information about your company, and products/services in which you may be interested.

- Enrolling in Frequent Buyer programs for such services as travel, lodging, car rentals, and even restaurant survey forms requesting additional personal information.

What are these companies doing with all of this information? Astute companies are using it to build complex and intricate databases. Database marketing is becoming a vitally important sales and marketing tool for many companies. It allows you to group your customers by individual purchases so you can properly target your advertising and promotional dollars. As a result, fewer companies are wasting money promoting to the masses and instead are spending money promoting to the audience most likely to purchase their specific product or service.

Effective database marketing requires an investment in sales and marketing technology. Central to this technology is an automated sales and marketing system, which allows you to build, manage and utilize a priceless marketing tool—your database.

Benefits of an Automated System

If properly implemented and utilized, an automated sales and marketing system will benefit your organization in the following areas:

- Sales performance
- Marketing effectiveness
- Operational efficiencies
- Administrative improvement.

Sales Performance

The automated sales and marketing system will greatly shorten the sales cycle by providing historical and competitive information that enables astute salespeople to upsell and employ value-added selling techniques. As a result, your salespeople will be better prepared to deal with clients and customers and able to focus their attention on areas that will produce the greatest results.

The automated system will also increase effective selling time. Computers reduce the time needed to complete daily tasks and give your salespeople more time to sell your products and/or services.

Marketing Effectiveness

An automated sales and marketing system will enable your organization to collect data and make more informed decisions, which will, in turn, improve sales and profitability. The automated sales and marketing system will help you:

- Improve lead generation and qualification by targeting prospects through specific media. Tying your automated system into strategic telemarketing activities can make your lead generation and qualification system produce qualified prospects for follow up by your sales team.

- Increase advertising and promotional effectiveness by helping you track the performance of your advertising and promotional efforts. The system will also allow you to capture pertinent marketing and demographic information provided by leads and prospects.

- Increase the quality of your customer service. The automated sales and marketing system is ideal for managing increasing amounts of prospect and customer information while enhancing communication with individual customers. When fully utilized, the system will provide improved levels of customer service and satisfaction.

Operational Efficiencies

The automated sales and marketing system can be an integral part of your total organization's operation and can help you attain greater efficiency. The system will allow you to:

- *Build a centralized database*—Why dissipate effort by stashing bits and pieces of data throughout your organization in many different formats? The automated system allows you to centralize information in standardized customer profiles.

- *Streamline the information flow*—Your automated database should be integrated with other information systems within your company to reduce duplicate information and increase efficiency of data collection and retrieval.

Administrative Improvement

Although the automated sales and marketing system is certainly not paperless, it can provide many administrative benefits for your organization. The system will help you:

- *Reduce paperwork*—The automated sales and marketing system allows information to be drawn from data that was entered only once. It also maintains records and files in an electronic format, reducing the need for physical storage systems.

- *Increase productivity*—The automated sales system reduces duplicate work, minimizes data entry and makes data retrieval quick and easy.

These benefits will help you know and understand your customers better, and the more you know about your customers, the more opportunities you have for increasing sales.

Implementing an Automated System

How can your organization implement an effective automated system and realize these benefits? You can automate your sales and marketing functions using a three-step process that includes planning, designing a system, and implementing your plan.

Step 1: Planning

- In the planning stage, you will carefully define your needs and establish goals and objectives to meet those needs.

Step 2: Designing a system

- In this step, you will consider your hardware and software needs and initiate training for those who will be using the system.

Step 3: Implementing the plan

- This step will allow you to see your automated sales and marketing system at work and enjoy its many benefits.

Let's take a closer look at this process.

Planning

The planning stage is crucial to the development of your automated sales and marketing system. As mentioned previously, you will determine your needs and establish guidelines for meeting those needs. Encourage everyone who will be affected by the new system to offer input about the plan. Then, once the plan is developed, document and communicate it to your entire organization. With a well-developed plan, you can effectively use your automated sales and marketing system to produce the results you want.

The following actions will help you understand your organization's particular needs and determine how you will meet them. It is essential that you:

- Define your sales process
- Conduct a needs assessment
- Establish goals and objectives.

Define Your Sales Process

The process of completing a sale or transaction is similar to taking a road trip. You have a starting point and an ending destination—in this case, the close of a sale, the payment of an invoice. Just as a vacation may include the use of a road map, the well-planned sales process serves as a guide to identify the major steps toward completion of a sale. Once you automate your sales process, you will be able to track your team's performance in these major areas:

- Lead generation
- Prospect qualification and rating
- Initial contact
- Sales calls
- Product/service demonstrations
- Proposals/quote presentations
- Contract/agreement/transaction acceptance
- Delivery/installation.

Once you have identified the major parts of your specific sales process, you can zero in on the critical selling activities of each part; these activities should contribute to the completion of that particular part of the sales process. For example, activities such as advertising, promotions, telemarketing, meetings, product demonstrations, reviewing bid specifications, issuing quotes or proposals, closing the sale, and delivering the product or service are all parts of the sales process that need to be accomplished.

Conduct a Needs Assessment on Your Own Company

You must assess your organization's sales and marketing needs in order to plan the proper sales and marketing automation system for your organization. Consider the marketing and selling activities in each major part of your sales process; then think about the areas of your organization that control those activities and plan how you will address the following needs:

- Human resources
- Physical resources
- Marketing.

Human Resources

All sales and marketing activities require people to complete certain operational tasks, such as managing the company's database, performing accounting functions, and controlling inventory and warehouse management activities.

Your new system may require additional staff or temporary help to fill in while your employees are learning the new system. Plan carefully before the system is in place. This will make the transition easier. A sufficient staff is crucial to the proper implementation and use of your automated sales and marketing system.

Also, consult your sales and marketing team. Will
you need project managers to relieve your salespeople of
non-selling tasks? Will you need additional salespeople
to handle new territories? Consider those involved in the
sales process itself and those who indirectly support each
part of your sales process.

Physical Resources

You cannot implement an effective sales and marketing program without first planning where you are going
to put all the computers and other equipment that the
process requires. Any additional staff you may hire will
require additional office space and supplies. Do you
have adequate office space? Do you have a phone line
for each person? Do you have a facsimile machine to
help speed information into and out of your organization? Do your salespeople require cellular phones to
communicate with your office and their customers?

As you will see later, it is absolutely necessary to
evaluate your computer system. The most effective
automated sales management systems operate on personal computers, or PCs. Will everyone have a computer on their desk or will they work on laptops? How
many printers will you need? Will you need additional
outlets and/or circuits? Where will the backed-up data
be stored? All of these questions must be answered
before your new system can run smoothly and
effectively.

Marketing

Because your marketing program plays a crucial role
in your overall sales process, it will be affected by your
automated sales and marketing functions as well. As
you plan how the two will work together, identify your
advertising and promotional program objectives. Are

you trying to generate leads or cultivate long-term accounts? How will you organize the information generated? Evaluate your historical and current data on customers and your product mix. This analysis will help you determine the ideal product mix for a particular customer segment.

Establish Goals and Objectives

Once you have identified the critical parts of your sales process and conducted a thorough needs assessment, the next step in the planning process is to set goals and objectives for improving your sales and marketing process through automation. Consider your needs carefully and set realistic and attainable goals. Remember budget considerations and personnel needs. Don't try to accomplish everything at once. Your automated system will develop over a period of time as everyone is trained and develops the skills to implement new procedures.

Designing a System

You are now ready to design an automated system that meets the specific needs of your sales and marketing organization. As you develop the system design, consider these five components:

- The database
- Hardware
- Software
- System support
- Training.

The Database

The database, which contains a summary of all prospect and customer information, is the heart of any automated sales and marketing system. The database information is especially important to your salespeople who can use it to gain confidence before calling on prospects and customers. This will quickly generate a higher level of rapport between salespeople and their customers, expediting the sales process.

The accuracy and integrity of your database is best maintained if the database is centralized. The database information is irreplaceable and invaluable to your organization. You have paid for it through sizeable sales and marketing expenditures over a period of time, and it should be protected at all costs. Locate your complete prospect and customer database in a central area, and assign one person to administrate the overall database and be responsible for every aspect of it. You will retain a higher level of database integrity if you follow established procedures for data input, output, maintenance and backup.

A centralized, automated database offers the highest level of protection from natural or historical deterioration, employee turnover and accident. The automated sales and marketing system also provides an excellent electronic method for long-term data storage and protection.

Your database should be standardized into customer and prospect profiles that provide consistent information from one record to the next. Each profile should contain standard information, such as contact name, title, and company name and address. The record may also include other information, such as an alternate contact name, a secretary's name, or a specific identification number.

The more specific the information you obtain for each customer profile, the better. This customized, or user-defined, information identifies the specific profile relative to its importance to your sales and marketing efforts. This may include the size of the company, its product and service needs, budget considerations, the authority of the contact to make the decision, competitive and historical information, or other applicable information regarding the purchase. By maintaining consistency between your profiles, you will utilize your database to its fullest potential to make strategic sales and marketing decisions.

Hardware

Automated sales management systems can operate on a variety of computer platforms or sizes. Here we will focus on automated sales and marketing systems designed for PC-based systems that operate on desktop or laptop models. It is recommended that the automated sales management system be built around an IBM or IBM-compatible hardware system.

Your primary hardware component will be the computer itself. Consider a computer equipped with 486 microprocessing capability for faster data processing, which will be increasingly important as your database grows. The computer should have a minimum hard disk storage capacity of 80 megabytes, providing storage capacity to input up to 1,500 customer profiles, activity information and other customer data.

Install a high-resolution, VGA-type monitor with a minimum screen size of 14-inches. This type of monitor is recommended for usage periods exceeding two hours. It is also best to invest in a color monitor so you can use your program and its various capabilities to the fullest extent.

Invest in a high-quality laser jet printer. The automated sales and marketing system can require large quantities of output, especially direct mail correspondence, and a laser jet printer will facilitate high-quality communications. When purchasing your printer, specify:

• An envelope attachment

• Label printing capability

• Various font selections

• Carriage size of at least 80 characters.

Whether to install desktop computers or laptop computers depends on your organizational structure. If you have field salespeople or external sales offices that need to share information, install laptops with identical specifications.

Laptops provide those who travel the functionality of an office away from the office. This is critical if decisions need to be made in the field that require access to the database. But never compromise the consistent maintenance and integrity of your central database, regardless of who may be accessing the information.

You may want to purchase internal modems, which are optional accessories used for data communication between other computers. Also, facsimile cards will allow you to fax documents directly from your computer.

Software

Contact management software is ideal for database management activities. It provides the capabilities for a centralized database and also facilitates the transfer of data for satellite database usage. It is the perfect software for the non-technical computer user, especially sales and marketing executives who lack computer experience.

Contact management software is an effective conduit to building your database, because it:

- Is inexpensive, usually costing less than $500, and sometimes even less than $200

- Is easy to install and operate

- Allows you to easily customize your customer profiles

- Facilitates a wide variety of direct marketing functions

- Produces custom reports

- Communicates with other software programs on your computer.

Many contact management programs are on the market today. Your automated sales and marketing system should utilize contact management software with the following requirements:

- A complete package with full user documentation

- A user-friendly, menu-driven system

- Standard information and user-defined information screens in each profile

- A complete calendar and scheduling system

- A mail merge feature to produce standardized correspondence

- A mailing label production feature.

Your automated sales and marketing system should be equipped with additional support software. This would include effective word processing software for producing correspondence and sales letters. You may also want to consider spreadsheet software for performing analytical tasks.

An electronic mail program is important if you have satellite databases on laptops. "E-mail" allows your database users to transmit information, data and correspondence between themselves via phone lines. This can speed up the decision-making process, especially in a decentralized organization.

System Support

A well-designed automated sales and marketing system cannot be effectively implemented and maintained without proper support, which includes technical service, marketing tools, and training. This support must be maintained throughout the life of your automated sales and marketing system.

As previously noted, the database administrator will be responsible for internal support of your database system. Technical service support for your system is usually provided by your dealer or distributor. You may have to access technical support through the manufacturer in some situations, however. Most hardware and software manufacturers do have support lines and technical assistance available at a nominal fee. Your database administrator should procure these services when necessary.

Marketing support, which will probably come from within your organization, includes the design and production of materials used to interact with your automated sales and marketing system. Marketing materials include sales call reports, customer profile printouts, procedures manuals, standard sales letters, customer surveys, proposals, and other marketing and correspondence materials.

"At this point in my report, I'll ask all of you to follow me to the conference room directly below us!"

Training

Training is a critical element in the success of your automated sales and marketing system. An effective training program should include theory, operating techniques and procedures.

Train those who will use the automated sales and marketing system on the benefits of the program. They must understand how it can improve the company's sales and the individual performance of sales and marketing professionals. They must also understand your organization's overall goals and objectives for implementing the system.

Operational training is simply learning how to use the system. The more your team knows about the operation of the system, the more likely they are to use the system to its maximum potential.

Procedural training outlines the step-by-step activities that must occur in order for the system to operate effectively. Procedures training will demonstrate how and why users must interact with the database on a continuous and consistent basis.

Implementing the Plan

You are now ready to fully implement your organization's plan for automating its sales and marketing process. Follow these guidelines as you begin this process.

Putting the System Into Action

*   Establish a thorough implementation schedule and time line. Follow the schedule one step at a time.

Trying to implement the entire system at once will be overwhelming and counter-productive.

- Install the system's components. As you prepare your facilities to accommodate the PC and all its associated hardware, consider accessibility, power requirements, time-sharing with other users, and security. After you have installed and customized the contact management software and any other necessary software, conduct preliminary tests with sample data to test the system and its capabilities. Make any necessary adjustments based on the results of your tests.

- Provide adequate training to ensure successful system implementation. First, provide training for the database administrator. Once this is done, your database administrator can then train all users and management.

- Load preliminary prospect and customer data. Begin with each salesperson's top 10 accounts and top 10 prospects.

- Track all major steps and the sales and marketing activity of the preliminary prospect or customer profiles. Use sales call reports and produce profile updates, weekly activity reports, weekly schedules and calendars, and any custom reports required to assess sales and marketing activities.

- Once you've satisfied all operating requirements for preliminary data, load all new leads and prospects onto the database. Track activity and produce custom reports, such as lead source analyses.

- Perform direct marketing functions associated with your sales and marketing activities. Produce and store standardized sales letters and perform a mail merge to personalize the letters based on completed sales and marketing activities. Also, conduct tele-marketing functions one to two weeks after the mailing, and track activity on the system. Produce a summary report to assess the success of your marketing activities.

- Evaluate the system after 30 days, including:

  - *Hardware and software*—Do they meet your needs and requirements?

  - *Database structure*—Does it meet your expectations and requirements?

  - *Training*—Was it adequate? Is additional or continuous training necessary?

  - *Overall effectiveness*—Are procedures to ensure database integrity in place and working effectively?

- Revise the system according to your evaluation results. Obtain input from your sales and marketing team on required changes, and work quickly to make the necessary revisions and get the system working efficiently.

- Integrate all facets of your automated sales system to incorporate lead generation and qualification, customer profile reports, sales activity reports and management reports.

Estimate at least one week for each of the main steps, which means the entire process will take at least four to six weeks to complete. Take as much time as is necessary to get the system operating to its full potential in all areas.

Measuring Performance

Your automated sales and marketing system must satisfy the goals and objectives that you have established. Recognizing the areas in which the system falls short of your goals and objectives will point the way for you to make necessary changes.

Usually, it is most practical to satisfy one goal or objective at a time. This helps your database administrator fully understand and appreciate the total capabilities of the system and gradually build it into an effective sales and marketing tool for your needs. As more goals and objectives are met, the overall performance of the system will increase and provide additional benefits to your organization.

All of those people who are either directly or indirectly affected by the automated sales and marketing system should have the opportunity to provide input in the evaluation process. What may not be evident to a direct user may impact the indirect user differently. For instance, leads from your advertising program may be getting keyed into the system satisfying the marketing department's goal of increased lead generation. However, if no follow-up report is provided on that lead, the actual sales results of the advertising program may never be known.

Implementing a Continuous Improvement Program

One important by-product of all new systems implemented within your organization should be an improvement in overall quality and service to your customers. Your automated sales and marketing system is no exception. Provide ways to ensure continuous improvement in the way that this system is utilized.

One way may be to include a performance survey with all invoices. Survey results can be tracked according to product line or service, and results of the survey can be keyed into the system. You can then evaluate your organization's performance by product and market segment.

Many companies provide creative ways to motivate their employees to continually improve individual performance and that of the total organization. Set up a suggestion system for all members of the organization. Pay special attention to suggestions from those interacting with customers who also use the database. Provide incentives to those directly using the data to maintain and update the data for accurate records. Also, look for ways to streamline the overall sales and marketing process via your new automated sales and marketing system.

The Rewards of Automation

Automating the sales process can be an exciting and rewarding investment for any organization fully committed to making the system work. But it is more than that. Automating the sales process is the key to remaining competitive as the global economy becomes more challenging for businesses everywhere. Companies who automate the sales process will keep pace with the best; those who neglect this critical function will lag further and further behind. The choice is yours. If you plan carefully, choose a system that meets your specific requirements, and utilize the system to its fullest potential, you will be rewarded with increased sales, more productive salespeople and loyal customers.

CHAPTER 4

MANAGING THE SALES PROCESS: THE SECRET TO INCREASING SALES

In today's competitive marketplace, it is more important than ever to manage your sales process effectively. Without a carefully laid plan for increasing sales and building strong customer relationships, you can lose your competitive edge, which will eventually impact your long-term viability.

In this chapter you will learn how to implement a successful sales management process. By following the suggestions listed here, you will:

- Establish your sales, gross profit, and market share objectives

- Increase the efficiency of your sales administration

- Control your sales expenses

- Develop an energized, successful sales force

- Implement specific sales tactics to maximize your available resources

- Achieve increased sales and build long-term customer relationships.

Companies, managers, and business owners are continually faced with sales and marketing problems that impact the bottom line. Typical problems include:

- High turnover of sales representatives

- Ineffective advertising campaigns

- Price and margin cutting to meet competition

- Stagnant product lines sold only through the use of incentives

- Lack of sales force accountability

- Disputes about territory and account assignments

- Dissatisfied customers and deteriorating relationships.

How do owners, managers and companies respond to these problems? Too often, they react to problems but fail to remedy them. Their reactions may include:

- Hiring more salespeople

- Firing salespeople

- Increasing the advertising budget

- Discounting prices

- Offering incentives

- Developing sales call reports

- Flying the management team out to visit customers.

Reactionary decisions produce inconsistent results that seldom meet long-term profit, market share and growth objectives.

For the past two decades, American businesses have concentrated on managing long-term performance by improving engineering, manufacturing, production, and distribution functions and processes. As the world marketplace becomes more competitive, it will become increasingly important for you to focus on managing your entire organization with emphasis on the marketing and sales process. In short, the secret to increasing sales is a managed, customer-focused sales process.

Managing sales is a fairly logical process. You can increase sales and meet long-term objectives by developing and implementing:

- A well-documented sales plan

- A well-defined organizational and administrative structure

- Innovative database management

- Effective sales tactics and strategies.

These components must work in conjunction with one another to build and strengthen your business so it is capable of withstanding economic and competitive pressures.

Sales Planning

You've probably heard the saying, "Plan your work and work your plan." This certainly holds true for sales planning. Therefore, work your sales plan by following this four-step process:

Step 1: Establish sales goals

- Sales goals give your organization a standard by which to measure performance.

Step 2: Establish budgets

- Budgets provide a cost-control mechanism to maximize profits.

Step 3: Identify your target market

- Your target market is comprised of companies, organizations, or individuals that have a need for your products and services and the desire and resources to purchase them.

Step 4: Establish sales strategies

- The key is to utilize your total resources to maximize sales and profit returns.

Let's take a closer look at these four components.

Sales Goals

Sales goals provide a necessary benchmark for measuring performance. Realistic and obtainable sales goals must take into consideration the resources you have to support these goals. For example: An annual sales goal of $1,000,000 would translate into 389 sales per year based on last year's average sale of $2,571. Yet last year the sales team brought in only 295 sales. What are you going to do to enable your salespeople to meet those higher objectives? You can add new products, provide value-added services to help increase the average sale, or you can increase the productivity of your salespeople by providing them with pre-qualified leads. The point is, you're going to have to do something different; you can't just issue a new goal, expecting they'll figure out a way to attain it.

Enable your salespeople to meet your objectives by establishing:

- *Monthly sales goals*—Consider seasonal demand and other factors that may affect your sales in any given month.

- *Monthly expense goals*—For every sale there is a cost of sale. Determine the point at which costs exceed profits, whether those costs are for media advertising, direct sales calls, direct mail or telemarketing. Certain products might not be profitable when sold by a direct sales force but might do very well when marketed through direct mail.

- *Monthly gross profit objectives*—These are sales minus cost of sales. They will determine the operating revenue for any given month.

Budgets

Once you have determined your sales goals, create a budget that effectively controls expenses and maximizes profit. Since certain resources must be allocated to the sales effort, it is important to establish the following budgets:

- *Personnel budget*—Ask yourself, "How many people does it take to generate an order and carry that order through the sales process?" Be sure to count sales executives, sales associates, customer service representatives and any other people required to complete the sale. At what point will you need to add people? At what level will it make sense to cut back?

- *Capital budget*—If you buy rather than lease, take into account the capital requirements to generate a sale:

  - Automobiles for your salespeople

  - Office and car telephone/fax services

  - Sales automation requirements.

  Consult your accountant to determine whether buying or leasing is better for your business.

- *Advertising and promotional budget*—Consider your target market when determining advertising and promotional expenses. If your target market consists of a few customers in a 300-mile radius, your advertising and promotional expenses will be very different from those of a company marketing products by mail to a nationwide audience. Also, consider seasonal or other characteristics that require additional expenditures.

Target Market

Ask yourself these questions:

- Who is my competition?

- Who are my prospects and customers?

- What limitations do I have in marketing to these prospects and customers?

- What industries or demographic groups do they represent?

- How large are these companies?

- How frequently do these customers buy our products? What triggers their decision to buy?

- Where are they located?

- Why are we interested in selling to certain organizations or individuals?

For help in answering these questions, complete the following steps:

Step 1: Develop a market analysis

- Identify the type of customers who have a need for your product mix. Companies are classified by Standard Industrial Classification codes, known as SIC codes. There are 11 industry SIC codes with hundreds of subclassifications. Typically, it is most effective to minimize the number of SIC codes that you target.

Step 2: Perform a competitive analysis

- Identify companies who are marketing and selling similar products and services within your market.

- Estimate your competition's sales and their market share.

- Compare your company and competition according to organizational structure, products and services.

- Determine your company's greatest strengths.

Step 3: Identify target accounts

- List prospects and customers that meet your market analysis requirements.

- Focus on prospects and customers with whom you have a competitive advantage.

- Categorize prospects and customers according to short- and long-term sales and profit potential.

Sales Strategies

Market strategies should focus on the basics, the Four P's of marketing: product, price, promotion and place. Let's take a closer look at these four elements.

Product Mix: The sum total of the products and services that you have available to sell.

- Identify product mix opportunities within your market for new customers. What else would these customers buy from you, if you made it available to them?

- Identify additional opportunities with existing customers.

- Balance product mix sales with your available resources to maximize profits. For example, you may be able to sell unlimited quantities of products requiring very little labor. But your own work force limitations may curtail the amount of services you can provide. Therefore, you must establish a balanced product mix to make optimum use of your available resources.

Price

- Establish prices to achieve balanced product mix objectives.

- Maintain sufficient margins to achieve long-term profit objectives.

- Build profits through value-added selling strategies, combining the sale of products and services with varying margins to achieve a higher margin on the total sale.

Promotion

- Plan advertising and promotional efforts to maximize demand for your product mix. Consider holidays, seasonal opportunities and other market influences.

- Increase promotional expenditures to maximize benefits from major events within your marketplace. Tie in with an open house, product introductions, sporting events or other local or regional celebrations.

Place

- Determine the geographical scope of your target market.

- Allocate available resources to market, sell and distribute your products and services within a national, regional or local marketplace.

Administration

Your company's philosophy on marketing, sales and customer satisfaction will determine the efficiency of your sales organization and its administration. Every person within your organization affects the sales process. What you deliver to your customers is the result of the combined efforts of everyone in your organization.

Improve your organization's ability to deliver a strategic product mix, and you will improve your sales performance. Increased efficiency and more effective administration throughout your organization contribute to profitable sales by:

- Reducing the costs of goods sold

- Reducing operating expenses

- Maintaining higher margins at lower prices

- Increasing demand through product improvement

- Improving distribution channels

- Increasing customer satisfaction and product demand

- Improving customer relationships and adding to their longevity.

The objective of the sales process is to maximize effectiveness and profits. Here are four components of a managed approach to the organization and administration of the sales process:

- Organizational structure

- Communications

- Training

- Compensation.

Organizational Structure

Your company's organizational structure needs to be well-defined in order to operate at peak performance. Everyone within your organization must be marching to the same beat to produce harmonious results for your company and your customers. This can be achieved by developing the following management tools:

• *Organizational chart*—Graphically illustrate the hierarchy of your company.

• *Position descriptions*—Document the responsibilities for each position listed on the organizational chart.

• *Work/Paper flow charts*—Graphically illustrate the flow of all paper generated or otherwise used for the sales process. Consider every document that is used to generate and complete a sale:

• Sales call reports	• Proposals
• Work order	• Purchase orders
• Product requests	• Invoices
• Acknowledgments	• Receipts
• Sign-off forms	• Requests for service
• Warranties	
• Authorizations to proceed	

Communications

Companies that are managed most effectively allow decisions to be made as close as possible to the source of the problem. Clear, open lines of communication into, within and out of an organization can speed up decision response rates, which can lead to increased customer satisfaction and sales.

"And then last week, I was feeling, oh . . . kind of unappreci-
ated, I guess . . . so I faked a system-wide data crash."

To produce effective communications for your company and customers, include or improve upon these
important elements in your company's organizational
structure: documentation, methods and procedures.

Documentation

Document each step of the sales process according
to your paper flow chart, including:

* Transactions

* Data collection

* Correspondence.

Methods

There are many simple yet innovative ways to enhance communication for your sales team, such as:

• *Bulletin boards and wall charts*—Post company-wide notices, sales results and miscellaneous communications on bulletin boards or charts.

• *Newsletters*—Communicate useful information periodically to employees, customers and prospects with a well-written, informative newsletter. Smaller organizations can enjoy the same benefits with less work by issuing Monday-morning bulletins.

• *Staff meetings*—Review progress, conduct short-term planning, discuss critical issues, and develop action steps at action-oriented staff meetings.

Enhance the accuracy and speed at which information flows internally and externally for your organization by using up-to-the-minute technology, such as local area networks (LANs) and electronic mail (E-mail). Companies that cannot afford to use the latest technology need to have appropriate forms on hand to promptly communicate routine information to other departments or individuals.

Procedures

Establish written communication procedures for each area of your business to help prevent disruptions in information flow and to ensure effective communications, responsible decision-making and accurate billing.

Training

If you expect top performance from your sales force, plan to invest time and money in a well-designed training program to motivate them toward achieving higher levels of performance. Management must determine training requirements for each level of the organization and research the many sales training courses available before committing to a specific program. To be effective, training must be organized and supported by management and receive buy-in from the sales team, too. Just as placing one ad doesn't maintain sales for a year, likewise, one training session won't maintain your sales force's enthusiasm and effectiveness for a year. An ongoing company-wide training program can provide excellent synergism throughout the organization, resulting in increased effectiveness for your sales process.

Requirements

Look for a program that meets the requirements of individual participants. Examine your sales force and assess individual needs by answering these questions:

- Are my salespeople young and inexperienced?

- How many of my employees are seasoned veterans?

- Which salespeople are primarily responsible for generating and closing new business?

- Which salespeople are assigned to building and maintaining relationships with existing accounts?

By answering these questions, you will be able to determine the type of program that will motivate and benefit individuals within your sales organization. The following chart depicts typical sales force requirements:

SALES TRAINING

Type of Sales Force	Areas for Training
Young, less experienced salespeople hired to generate new business.	Sales Techniques Presentation Skills Product Training
Seasoned sales force responsible for handling major customer assignments.	Relationship Selling Account Development Value-added Selling

---

Studies have shown that higher levels of training directly correlate with higher performance levels. Your salespeople will close more sales if they have the knowledge and skills to meet the customers' requirements.

Sources

There are several sources of training that can be tailored to meet your organization's requirements:

- *Consulting and training organizations*—Check your Yellow Pages or call the local chapter of American Society for Training and Development.

- *Manufacturers*—Many large organizations offer product marketing and sales programs that meet most requirements of their distribution network.

- *Community organizations*—These include the Chamber of Commerce, Employer's Association and other professional groups.

- *Continuing education programs*—Universities, colleges and community colleges are all excellent sources for training.

Compensation

People who enjoy their work, are happy with their work environment, and believe they are compensated fairly are also motivated. It is management's role to provide these conditions for all workers and to avoid demotivating them. This is especially true with your sales force.

Salespeople respond favorably to well-designed incentive programs. Here are a few suggestions for building a successful incentive program based on an interview with Hugh Aaron of Belfast, Maine. Aaron is a frequent writer for *The Wall Street Journal* and a former supplier to the plastics industry.

- Make the incentive worth pursuing.

- Give the incentive often—once a month is good. "People want immediate gratification," Aaron says, "and the younger they are, the more they want it."

- Keep the lines of communication open. Meet with them. Encourage them. Give them what they need to make sales.

- Tie the incentive to productivity, not profits. "That's management's responsibility," notes Aaron.

Structure

Most likely, 80 percent of your business comes from 20 percent of your accounts. Therefore, staff appropriately to generate 80 percent of your sales, not to call on 80 percent of your accounts.

Different types of salespeople are motivated by different types of compensation structures. Ask yourself what type of compensation structure is best for each particular salesperson. Examine your sales force by the total compensation that you can afford and the type of salesperson that you have:

- *Sales maintainers*—Maintainers are the people you should assign to long-term, high-volume accounts, where high levels of expertise and professionalism are required to ensure strong, healthy business relationships. A sales maintainer may be comfortable drawing a salary supplemented by a bonus program.

- *Sales closers*—Closers actively pursue and qualify leads and increase your sales through new business contacts and relationships. They're more often motivated by a generous commission structure.

Sales Tactics

You've developed your plan, established your goals and defined your sales organization. Your sales team is in place, ready to go and make it happen. Now, how do you empower them to meet their goals and objectives?

There are four simple but effective tactics you can implement to make the best possible use of all these resources:

- Build consistent sales with existing accounts.

- Generate new sales by penetrating a highly targeted market.

- Practice value-added selling for your complete product mix.

- Commit to continuous improvement.

These simple tactics fit very well into a wide variety of organizations. The key is to assess the potential gain from each of these tactics and to implement management practices focused on maximizing this potential. Let's examine each of these tactics in more detail.

Build Consistent Sales with Existing Accounts

Your goal in building sales with existing accounts should be building and maintaining long-term sales relationships. It is important to generate a consistent level of sales in order to protect your organization from the peaks and valleys of a typical sales cycle caused by economic, seasonal factors and various other reasons. As the marketplace becomes more competitive, this tactic is essential to maintaining your business base.

There are several keys to successfully building sales with existing accounts:

•   Make servicing existing accounts the No. 1 priority for designated salespeople. Customers are looking for reliable, buyer-seller relationships. It's important that you stay in close touch with people—even if they have just bought from you—so you're in tune with their special circumstances and you're there when they need you.

•   Establish procedures that ensure periodic follow-up with these customers. Think about the people you know that have left previous customers and gone on to other opportunities in your target market. Contact them again; explain why you have a special interest in them. Tell them about new products and services that will appeal to them. Ask what you can do to earn their business.

•   Establish a communication program specifically for these clients. This program could include newsletters, phone calls, marketing bulletins, sales letters, holiday cards, or handwritten notes. Whatever you do, make it a program, not a one-time effort.

- Keep the competition at bay and minimize the discounting of your profit margin by keeping your existing customers happy with your company's products and services.

Generate New Sales by Penetrating a Highly Targeted Market

This tactic is important because new customers:

- Provide new sources of revenue

- Help build the awareness of your organization and product mix

- Help identify the true needs for your products and services within the marketplace

- Can become long-term clients.

There are several ways to implement a successful new-sales generation program:

- Assign your most aggressive sales team members to the task of generating leads and sales. Some companies perform sales blitzes in target areas where all of their sales efforts are focused on generating new business for a specific period of time.

- Polish your company image. Make sure your company and your sales team project an image of professionalism—service—reliability.

- Establish and implement a systematic communication program that builds awareness of your company with your target market. This program could include direct mail, telemarketing, and targeted advertising and promotion.

- Increase your promotional efforts and maintain a consistent message—always communicating your competitive edge over and over again in everything you do.

- Look for market niches and new opportunities. Strive to become the solution your customers have been looking for and serve as an outstanding supplier to them in that special area.

- Invite prospects to special events you are sponsoring, such as seminars, open houses, and trade show exhibits. Create a dialogue; get to know them. Then stay in touch with them on a regular basis. How long? Forever.

Practice Value-Added Selling for Your Complete Product Mix

Increasing market share requires increased sales, but that's only half the equation. Growth can take place only when there is sufficient profit to support added resources and selling efforts. That is why value-added selling is so important: it helps you maintain your profit objectives while aggressively pursuing new sales.

Stretching additional resources to meet competitive challenges, especially for any one product, erodes profit margins. Profit margins for a particular sale can be maintained, however, and even increased, if you package products and services together to maintain a higher margin. This is value-added selling.

Many manufacturing and large retail chains actively and aggressively practice value-added selling.

Examples include:

- Extended warranties on automobiles and appliances
- Accessories sold with a base product

- Product upgrades

- Point-of-purchase selling.

These are all ways that you can build margins when the base or primary product contributes very little to the overall profit.

Commit to Continuous Improvement

Maintaining customer satisfaction through a company-wide commitment to continuous improvement can lead to increased sales. This process can be established at all levels of the organization and can improve:

- Your company's work environment

- The products and services you deliver

- Customer satisfaction and referrals

- Profits and long-term growth.

Many companies have instituted a continuous improvement process through their manufacturing, distribution and customer service functions. It is equally important to apply continuous improvement to the way you sell your products. Remember, customers form their opinions about your company by their interaction with one or more people at your company.

Consider adding these continuous improvement processes to your own sales process:

- Implement a systematic lead generation program that reduces cold calling by your salespeople. In some organizations, this can mean a cost savings of over $200 per cold sales call. For a tenth of that cost, you could send a series of letters and a brochure over a period of several weeks.

- Automate your database and sales management function. This process will help streamline the flow of paper required for each sale. In addition, automating your database and sales management function will increase time spent with customers, increase customer awareness of your company, and ultimately result in more opportunities for sales and profit.

- Establish procedures for every step of your sales process. These procedures can include guidelines for follow-up correspondence, activity reports, sales correspondence, customer billing and collections, generating proposals and presenting quotes.

- Train your salespeople to make every call count by focusing on customer needs, asking smart questions, acting as a problem solver to buyers, and helping create solutions for increased profitability.

Everyone in your organization should commit to continuous improvement. Many companies have established formal quality improvement programs and reward systems that motivate workers to do just that. Small rewards to your team can produce much larger rewards for the organization through increased sales and long-term customer relationships.

Implementing a Successful Sales Process

The secret to increasing sales is a well-managed, customer-focused sales process that includes sales planning, administration and sales tactics. As you plan your sales process with your sales team, be sure that your plan is in accordance with the organization's goals and objectives. Adjust your plan if necessary. Also, consider your available resources and plan accordingly.

Select market areas where you can be most successful, and concentrate your selling efforts on those areas.
As you consider avenues for marketing your product,
evaluate your target market, your product mix and your
competition. Finally, commit to specific sales tactics.
Consider the personalities of your salespeople and
implement strategies that will maximize the available
talents of your employees. Also, train your salespeople
to employ proven sales tactics and reward them for their
success.

If you implement these three steps, you will increase
sales and enjoy additional benefits of increased sales:
fewer peaks and valleys, a more stable work force and
stronger customer relationships.

CHAPTER 5
HOW TO WRITE BUSINESS PROPOSALS LIKE A PRO

Until a few years ago, the typical business proposal was little more than a price quote and a paragraph or two of sketchy details. Then as technology advanced and competition intensified, project management expertise and overall competence became as critical to the purchasing decision as basic cost considerations. These changes led to the need for more sophisticated proposals.

Today, proposals have become the basis for major purchasing decisions and for selecting qualified vendors. They are the primary means a company has for comparing products, services, ideas and credentials of one organization to those of its competitors. And yet, as important as proposals are, few business people have mastered the art of writing effective ones.

Why It Pays to Improve Your Proposal Writing Skills

A well-written proposal can:

- Enhance your professional image

- Enhance the image of your company

- Set you apart from your competition, especially if your proposal shows an understanding of the client's needs and proposes solutions

- Increase your prospective client's confidence in you by spelling out exactly what you will do, how you will do it, and all other details important to closing the sale

- Convey your competence in handling a particular assignment, enabling you to ask for—and receive—more compensation.

In this chapter, we will show you specific ways to write, polish and package your proposals for maximum salability. By sending out comprehensive, well-written proposals and cover letters, both you and your company stand to gain more sales than ever before. You'll also establish yourself as a competent resource, laying the groundwork for handling future projects.

What Exactly Is a Proposal?

A proposal is a formally written document containing facts and figures about a specific service or transaction to be provided, pending the reader's approval. It is drafted to meet the needs of a specific customer and includes:

- A complete description of the product or service to be provided

- A firm price quote

- A specified delivery date

- A specified mode of transportation.

In a well-written proposal, nothing is left to chance; nothing is open to question or misinterpretation. In fact, a well-written proposal is used initially to make a sale; but this same document is referred to after the sale is made, should questions or disagreements arise. Either party need only go back to the original signed proposal to verify the terms of the agreement.

Why It Pays to Write a Proposal

The purpose of writing a proposal is to provide a factual document for prospective customers to use as a basis for making an important buying decision. Proposals from more than one vendor are often solicited for the purpose of comparison. This comparison often takes place behind closed doors by a committee of several people who may not have had direct contact with the person or company submitting the proposal.

Proposals give decision-makers the opportunity to compare advantages and differences of one company's products or services to another company's based on facts rather than on a sales representative's presentation.

Your proposal must represent you and your company so well that it can make the sale even in your absence. It must be well-organized and easy to read. It must state complete details of the offer, persuasively and convincingly, and it must be attractively presented in order to close the sale.

Here are four other reasons it pays to write a proposal:

- Writing a proposal requires you to think through every facet of the job, every expense you will incur, the amount of your own time that will be involved and the amount of other people's time or services you'll need to buy before you can deliver what the client is expecting. Without the discipline of actually working through the details, it's too easy to misjudge or oversimplify the amount of work to be done and the costs involved. People who provide job estimates rather than proposals often end up with unhappy clients. Job estimates, which sound appealing then expand as the job progresses, often cause disputes, ill will and even court battles.

- Writing a proposal gives you the opportunity to communicate your understanding of the client's needs and to outline the approach you believe needs to be taken. Your face-to-face meetings may get you in front of only one person; your proposal, on the other hand, will more likely pass before the ultimate decision-makers.

- When you write a proposal and the prospective client agrees to it, the proposal becomes the basis of each party's expectations. If you state in your proposal that you will deliver "a 3-color brochure on 80-pound glossy card stock fanfolded so the address panel is exposed, flat measurement $8\frac{1}{2}$" x 11", there is little chance that the client will be expecting something else.

- After you have written your proposal, take the time to review it to make sure you've convinced the prospect of the need to say "Yes." The idea is to sell the benefits of accepting your proposal without giving the client a blueprint to do the job without your help.

When Writing a Proposal Is a Waste of Time

Beware of those who move quickly and ask for a proposal too soon after your initial contact with them. Such prospects are frequently gathering information from several sources to get ideas they can pass off as their own to impress a manager or co-worker. Too often, these prospects have no intention of buying anything.

You can avoid being used by people like this by asking qualifying questions first, then deciding whether or not a proposal is warranted.

Sample qualifying questions include:

- Is this a priority item for you?

- What is your timetable for implementing this service? installing this equipment?

- How much have you budgeted for this project?

- Who else will share in making this decision?

If you determine the prospect isn't ready for a proposal, maintain interest by writing a simple proposal letter in which you request a meeting with several people to more fully assess the company's needs. Provide information in your letter about what you can do and the benefits of working with your company. Tell the prospect you would like to work with them, and promise a detailed quote after you've met with their group and fully understand their needs.

Three Types of Proposals and When to Use Each One

The Letter Proposal

The letter proposal is simply a letter stating what one individual or company is willing to provide for another, when it can be provided, the price to be charged, and how payment for the product or service will be received. A letter proposal is appropriate when the product or service to be rendered is very simple.

(See Sample Proposal 1 on page 109.)

A Detailed Proposal for a Short-term Project

This type of proposal is recommended when the client may not be aware of the many steps involved in completing an assignment, such as in the development of a brochure. The company providing the service needs to spell out the details so the client has a written record of exactly what is included in the quote and what services could incur additional charges.

Because this type of proposal is very detailed, it is recommended that you make it easier for the client to read by using appropriate headings and bullet points such as:

Assignment: To design and produce . . .

Objective: To design a printed piece for generating qualified leads . . .

Project will include:

* Concept development, writing, graphic design . . .

* Copywriting of the six-panel brochure, cover letter and . . .

* Design, graphics, typesetting and keylining of . . .

Timetable:

Quantities and Proposed Price:

5M Brochures	$_____
5M Sheets of coordinated letterhead	_____
5M #10 envelopes	_____
5M #9 return envelopes	_____
Total	$_____

Terms and Other Details:

- A $\frac{1}{3}$ deposit with the signed Authorization is required . . .

- The second $\frac{1}{3}$ is due . . .

- The final $\frac{1}{3}$ is due . . .

Today's date:

It is also helpful to include a statement such as, "We will hold open time in our schedule and honor this proposal as written, adjusting the completion date as necessary, if returned by . . ."

(See Sample Proposal 2 on page 110.)

A Detailed Proposal for a Long-term Assignment

Other publications give a full explanation of how to write a detailed proposal for a long-term assignment. Such an explanation is beyond the scope of this book. In general, however, proposals for long-term assignments involve all of the tasks required for short-term assignments, with these additions:

- A thorough needs assessment

- A detailed procedures description including how you will interact with a client's management team

- Project time line

- Flow chart(s)

- Evaluation and reporting plan

- Capability statement

- Statement of assurances

- Supporting documents

- Cancellation clauses.

For further information on this type of proposal, refer to *How to Succeed as an Independent Consultant* by Herman Holtz (John Wiley & Sons, 1988) and *The Successful Consultant's Guide to Fee Setting* by Howard L. Shenson (The Consultant's Library, 1986).

Six Items Every Proposal Should Include

Every proposal, regardless of type, should include:

- A detailed description of the product or service to be provided

- A timetable for delivery of the product or service described

- The price with appropriate detail or breakdown of components

- Terms for payment

- Length of time the prospect has to accept the proposal

- Place for the prospect to sign his/her authorization to proceed.

- Cancellation clause (optional).

Writing the Actual Proposal

How Proposal Writing Differs From Other Kinds of Writing

Proposals are more formal than most letters. Most proposals are also technical documents, even if they describe non-technical products or services. They list facts, figures, times, prices and other specifics. Proposals can be legally binding if there is a dispute so it pays to write them with a great deal of thought and consideration of all consequences.

Even though proposals are technical by nature, they must also market your products or services. Therefore, you need to provide all the data required and, at the same time, sell the client on the idea of accepting your proposal.

To avoid misinterpretation, be sure to provide a working definition of terms that might be unclear to your reader. For example, your proposal might include a statement such as, "Design includes concept development, graphic design, color and paper selection, and total coordination with all other pieces in the package. Also included in the price is one set of camera-ready art. Additional stats, if needed, will be billed separately." Does your client understand what stats are?

Writing the proposal comes after you've listed all tasks involved and calculated all amounts and expenses that will enter into your total price. If others will be involved in the work described, have them review and give input on the draft.

Sitting Down to Write the Proposal

First, decide which type of proposal best suits your needs. Then write down the prospect's greatest problem (i.e., the organization's reason for seeking your assistance). Write down your primary selling point; this should be identical to your prospect's reason for seeking your assistance. Next, jot down the main points or headings you will want to include in your proposal. Leave the cover letter for last. Refer to the sample proposals on pages 109 to 112 if you need help getting started.

Filling in the Missing Information

Using the information you have, begin to fill in facts and information under the various headings. What other information do you need to provide?

Draw a simple flow chart on paper to help you think through the various steps involved in completing the client's project. This will help you identify additional information you'll need to include in your proposal.

What outside help or services will you need to employ to complete what you're promising? What expenses are you likely to incur that need to be included? Telephone? Transportation? Meetings? Postage, Federal Express or fax charges?

Once you have the facts, figures and supporting information, go to work to put everything together into a smooth, flowing document. Then, if possible, put it away for a day. Don't even think about it. Before you pick it up again, make a list of questions from the customer's perspective, asking everything someone in their business might want to know before making a purchasing decision.

Now go back to your document to make sure you've answered all those questions. As you reread it, you'll think of other things you've forgotten. Add them now. Work to smooth out the rough edges. Think of the marketing aspects; build in credibility. Build in some "sell."

Write your cover letter before doing your final polishing. That way any last-minute changes you think of as you write the letter can be easily inserted into your final draft of the proposal.

How to Pack Persuasion Into Your Cover Letter

The cover letter that accompanies your proposal is also a sales letter. Even though your proposal will be primarily factual, your cover letter needs to be persuasive and more personal. Your cover letter can give your proposal that extra edge that will persuade the reader to respond.

By the time you're asked to submit a proposal, you've been in contact with the customer enough to understand the organization's needs. List those needs on paper before you begin to write. Then write the letter to acknowledge the reader's needs. Answer the customer's unspoken question, "What's in this for me?" Build your message on the benefits of saying "Yes!" to your proposal.

Think about the person to whom you're writing your letter. This will help you custom-tailor your message. Your letter and proposal will probably be only one of many items crossing the decision-maker's desk and placing demands on his or her time. Your letter may be far more important to you, the seller, than to the reader who will be buying. You will choose your words carefully and edit your original draft. The reader will probably glance at it once before rushing past it to the proposal. Still, it's important that the letter be well written .

Also think about the purpose of your letter, which is to persuade the reader to accept your proposal. List the points you wish to make. Then select the one most important idea. This idea should express the greatest benefit of accepting your proposal, and it should mirror the client's greatest wish. Base your proposal on what the client hopes to achieve from your product or service, and be certain you can provide all that you propose.

More than likely, several people will review your letter and proposal, perhaps people you have had no contact with whatsoever. So make sure your letter projects a positive image of you and your company. Make certain that it conveys good will and interest in meeting the client's needs. Check to see that your letter shows you understand and care about those needs.

After you've written your letter, check it once more to see if you've:

- Stated the purpose of your letter clearly in the opening sentence

- Kept the letter brief, conversational and professional

- Made certain every detail of the letter is correct, especially the name, title, company name and all spellings

- Put a call to action in the last paragraph

- Ended with Sincerely or another appropriate close

- Made the letter look easy to read, leaving at least a one-inch margin on all sides and using short paragraphs

- Corrected all spelling and grammatical errors. (Ask a second person to proofread the letter again).

Polishing Your Proposal

If possible, have a person with editing capabilities assist you with polishing your cover letter and proposal. By now, you've been working with these documents a long time. Getting another person's input—a fresh perspective—can be extremely helpful.

After you've inserted all your changes and polished it until it shines, proofread it twice. Make final changes. You're now ready to package your proposal.

Packaging Your Proposal for Maximum Salability

You have invested a great deal of time and energy in writing your proposal and cover letter; there's a lot rid-

ing on its acceptance. Find out how many originals of the proposal the client will need. This inquiry provides an added bit of customer service on your part and also ensures that every person will receive a high-quality original, not a set of photocopies stapled in the corner.

Think of how much you've invested in preparing this proposal; don't let up now. Package it to beat the competition.

- Print each cover letter on your company letterhead.

- Hire someone with desktop publishing capabilities to produce a cover sheet, titles, headings, bullets and borders to dress up your report.

- Provide flow charts or graphs, in color, if possible.

- Print each proposal on quality paper—no photocopies.

- Enclose each proposal in an attractive binding or folder color-coordinated with your letterhead and business card.

- If you are mailing the proposals, be certain that the envelope, mailing label, stamp and seal are all compatible with the importance of the contents.

- Make certain the amount of postage is adequate so the envelope is not delivered with "Postage Due."

Your Key to Making the Sale

Anyone can jot down a few figures on a sheet of stationery and call it a proposal. But to write a proposal that is comprehensive—one that stands apart from the competition—one that makes the sale and wins the client's confidence—takes patience and skill. Remember: Your proposal could be the single greatest factor in determining whether or not you win the job. Make it shine.

Sample Proposal 1

December 17, 1993

Michael Roberts
XYZ Consulting Firm
12345 Woodcrest
Cleveland, OH 54321

Dear Michael:

Yesterday, I met with our graphics manager to review our telephone conversations and your objectives for the new proposal and capability statements for your firm.

We reviewed the mailing pieces you wish to replace and discussed significant improvements we could make to meet your objectives and expectations. We gave specifications to our printer and requested a quote on the quantities you specified.

We're pleased that we can write, design, print and deliver the following within your budget of $7,000 to $8,000:

- 500 folders on 80# colored cover stock, die-cut to form inside pockets with slits for a business card. The cover would be blind embossed with your logo.

- 500 each of 6 different inserts on 100 lb. text in three PMS colors.

- 2,500 4" x 8½" brochures with blind embossed covers and 8 inside pages printed in 3 colors on 100 lb. glossy stock.

If, after discussing this with your marketing director, you would like to proceed, I will provide you with a formal proposal.

Thank you for this opportunity. We look forward to working with you on this project. You can count on us to give you our very best.

Sincerely,

Sharon Winters

Sharon Winters

Sample Proposal 2

HIGH-IMPACT MARKETING SERVICES
2505 E. PARIS ROAD SE, SUITE 130
GRAND RAPIDS, MI 49546

PROPOSAL FOR CUSTOMER SURVEY
ABC MANUFACTURING, INC.
RACINE, WISCONSIN

ABC Manufacturing has asked High-Impact Marketing Services to provide and conduct a two-page Customer Survey to assess their customers' perceptions of ABC Manufacturing's quality. This proposal is based on meetings with Mary Mackie of High-Impact and John Crawford of ABC Manufacturing on November 12 and December 17. Attending the second meeting were Mary Mackie of High-Impact and the following representatives of ABC Manufacturing: John Crawford, Scott Veltman, Melissa McCormick, Mike Malone and Richard Wolcott.

Objectives of Conducting a Customer Survey:

ABC Manufacturing's primary objective in conducting this survey is to gather baseline data for determining whether a quality program will improve customers' perceptions of ABC Manufacturing. A secondary objective is to let customers know "We care."

Specifications:

The survey is to be printed on 11" x 17" 80 lb. white text stock with simple desktop publishing enhancements, including use of an attractive typeface. The questions will be printed only inside the folded survey and will be limited to two 8 $\frac{1}{2}$" x 11" panels. The outside front panel will identify the survey and carry the name ABC Manufacturing, Inc. The ABC Manufacturing Quality Statement will appear on the back outside panel of the document. No information will appear on the surveys or mailing envelopes to imply third-party involvement.

Number of surveys to be mailed: 1,000

ABC Manufacturing Areas of Responsibility:

- ABC will select the individuals and companies that are to receive the surveys. ABC will then provide High-Impact

ABC Manufacturing Proposal, page 2

with mailing labels. High-Impact will place the return
envelopes in the customer envelopes addressed to the various subsidiaries of ABC Manufacturing, Inc.

High-Impact Areas of Responsibility:

- High-Impact will write, edit, format and print the survey.
All expenses related to this effort (including telephone calls,
faxes and mailings) originating from High-Impact will be
covered by High-Impact. (Federal Express charges will be
billed to the party requesting the service.)

  The survey will be submitted to John Crawford three times
before it goes to print (first draft, revised draft, printer-ready
copy). Changes made after the final approval to print may
incur additional costs.

- High-Impact will provide #10 return envelopes that will be
pre-addressed to ABC Manufacturing.

- High-Impact will provide first-class postage for all customer
surveys and postage on all survey return envelopes.

- High-Impact will provide all labor and supervision con-
nected with stuffing, stamping and mailing the surveys.

- High-Impact will key in data for all surveys returned.

- High-Impact will write, edit and produce 12 copies of the
survey report for ABC Manufacturing executives. The
reports will include an Executive Summary, composite data,
and information specific to each subsidiary. All 12 reports
will be delivered in loose-leaf notebooks and will include
raw data, percentages, statistical data, narrative comments,
charts and/or graphs, interpretations and recommendations.

- High-Impact will produce up to 25 sales reports, which will
include an Executive Summary and an overview of each
respective division's survey results. These reports will contain only highlights so that the Vice President of Sales may
present information to the group as he sees fit. All information in these reports will be extracted selectively from the
president's reports and will contain no new information.

- High-Impact will present the survey findings at ABC corporate headquarters to key people invited by ABC. This presentation will be made approximately two weeks prior to the
company's annual sales meeting in April.

Cost $8,887

Today's date: December 29, 1993

AUTHORIZATION TO PROCEED

On behalf of ABC Manufacturing, Inc., I hereby authorize High-Impact Marketing Services to begin work described in their proposal of December 29, 1993.

It is my understanding that prices for all work quoted are firm, but that High-Impact will add or delete services with appropriate price modifications. I further understand that work not covered in the proposal, such as changes made after work has been approved, will incur additional charges if such work or changes are requested by ABC Manufacturing.

I understand that if, for any reason, ABC Manufacturing chooses to cancel this project before it is completed, that they agree to pay for expenses incurred and/or work completed, at High-Impact's regular hourly rate.

Our one-third deposit accompanies this agreement; 50% of the balance will be due before the survey is mailed, and the final balance will be due within 30 days of High-Impact's presentation of the survey report to key employees of ABC Manufacturing. One and one-half percent interest per month will be charged on amounts due past 30 days.

Deposit enclosed: $ _____

_____   _____
Authorized Signature   Date

CHAPTER 6
JOB DESCRIPTIONS
THAT REALLY WORK

Do you ever ask yourself, "Why aren't people doing their jobs?" or "What does it take to get people to respond—to feel a sense of urgency about the things that are important to the company?" Next time you reach your internal boiling point with these or similar frustrations, ask yourself, "Does each employee really understand his or her job responsibilities?"

Are your expectations of each employee consistent with the individual's job description? If several months or even years have passed since you've compared an employee's performance with his or her duties and responsibilities as stated in that person's job description, then it's time to pull it out, dust it off and read it carefully. Then meet with the employee. Start the meeting by giving praise for the duties and responsibilities being performed as expected and discuss openly those in need of improvement. Let the job description serve as the basis for possible changes, both in the job description itself and in the employee's performance.

No organization can afford to operate without well-written job descriptions. That's because a well-written job description:

- Provides documentation of each employee's job status, title and job function

- Provides a blueprint for each person's duties and responsibilities

- States the reporting relationship of this individual to others, clarifies who within the company the

employee interfaces with, and lists the external contacts the person may expect to have

- Lists the skills and abilities required for the position
as well as the education and experience needed for
an individual to qualify for the position

- May provide information on one or more positions
the individual could logically move into next.

The job descriptions for an organization include all
the tasks and responsibilities necessary for the entire
organization to function efficiently. And all relate to
meeting the organization's objectives; so theoretically, if
all employees follow their job descriptions, all objectives
will be met.

Consider the alternative. Suppose a company
attempts to operate without written job descriptions.
Reporting relationships are fuzzy; duties and responsibilities are unclear. If objectives are nonexistent or not
communicated, the chances of meeting goals are greatly
reduced and opportunities for true leadership simply
don't exist.

What's Included in a Job Description

A job description, a formal written document usually
one to three pages long, includes:

- Date it was written or issued

- Job status (exempt or non-exempt*, full-time or
part-time)

- Position title

- Supervision received (to whom the person reports)

*Exempt employees are those who are not eligible for overtime
compensation.

"Warm a chair . . . Swill coffee . . . Thumb through catalogues . . . By golly, Ted, he's RIGHT. They're all here in his job description!"

- Supervision exercised (who reports to this employee)

- Job summary (a synopsis of the job responsibilities)

- Principal contacts (inside and outside the company)

- Essential job functions

- Non-essential job functions

- Physical and mental competency requirements of the position

- Education/experience required for the position

- Career mobility, i.e., position(s) employee may qualify for next (optional)

- Regular meetings to attend and/or reports employee is expected to file (optional).

(See pages 129 to 138 for sample job descriptions.)

Writing Job Descriptions

Job descriptions may be written by someone in the personnel department or the department where the employee will be working. Writing job descriptions is a monumental task but one that is necessary for the efficient operation of any organization. The task will be more manageable if you begin by drawing an organizational chart of the company. This graphic representation of the reporting relationships will serve as a point of reference.

Once you've drawn the organization chart, use the sample form provided on page 131 and fill in the appropriate information for each position. Begin at the lowest levels of the organization and work toward the top, filling in the information as you go. You will want to complete the job descriptions for an entire department at one time so you can insert tasks and responsibilities in the appropriate places. Make sure every task is assigned to someone whose competence and skills match the work.

If, in the job descriptions, you have included that employees are to attend regularly scheduled meetings, ask yourself:

- Who is to schedule the meeting?
- Who is to arrange the meeting place?
- Who is to notify the people expected to attend?
- Who is to conduct the meeting?
- Who else is to directly participate on a regular basis?

Laws and Regulations Relating to Job Descriptions

Before you begin writing any job descriptions, become familiar with federal and state regulations that relate to employment. The federal government and every state have laws that employers must adhere to when writing job descriptions, hiring and terminating any employee. Your options may be further restricted if you are a unionized organization.

One of the most recent rulings regarding employment is the Americans with Disabilities Act (ADA). As of July 26, 1992, employers with 25 or more employees (15 or more beginning July 26, 1994) are required to look at potential employees as individuals with abilities and skills, not disabilities. The ADA prohibits disability discrimination and requires employers to reasonably accommodate those with disabilities so they can perform necessary job functions.

For maximum protection, the job description should be written before posting notice of a job opening, placing a classified ad or interviewing job applicants. This document can then provide valuable evidence should a dispute arise. Make certain the job description is up-to-date and accurate and that all aspects of the job are included. Under the ADA, the job description should include the following:

- Detailed description of essential job functions
- Knowledge, skills and abilities required
- Physical qualifications
- Mental qualifications.

You may not make pre-employment inquiries about an applicant's disability, only about his or her ability to perform specific work-related tasks. If you ask an applicant to show that he or she can perform a specific task, then you must make identical requests of all applicants.

Questions to Avoid During Interviews

Under all circumstances, avoid asking questions that pertain to:

- Conditions, illnesses or diseases

- Hospitalization

- The number of days missed on a previous job due to illness

- Conditions limiting an individual's ability to perform certain tasks

- Use of prescription drugs.

Essential Job Functions

Essential job functions, according to the ADA, are those which the employee should be able to perform on his or her own or with "reasonable accommodation." Essential job functions include those tasks that require a large percentage of the employee's time, those which, if not done, could bring dire consequences to the organization, and those considered integral to the performance of current or previous employees in the same position. If a duty can easily be performed by another employee, such as passing out the mail, then it is a non-essential function. Under the ADA, candidates unable to perform non-essential job functions cannot be disqualified from the hiring process since these duties can be reassigned to other employees within the organization.

Whether a job function is essential or non-essential depends on the nature of each position. Begin by analyzing the position. Why does the job exist? What does the job entail? How is the job successfully performed? Talk to supervisors and current or previous employees who have held the job. However you go about it, evaluate each job objectively and consistently. Devise a standard format for all job descriptions or use the ready-to-complete forms at the end of this chapter.

By writing job descriptions before recruiting, selecting and hiring—and including all of the above information into the process—you can help prevent potential legal problems and also ensure that you've hired the right person.

Utilizing Job Descriptions

Job descriptions provide documentation of current employees' respective positions within the company, their responsibilities, their supervisors and the employees who report to them. Job descriptions also identify those people who employees interface with inside and outside the company.

Under the headings "Essential Job Functions" and "Non-essential Job Functions," each item should be written so that it begins with a carefully chosen verb that clearly defines the degree of authority. For example:

- Recommends new vendors for all production materials.

- Prices, selects and orders all non-printed paper supplies for administrative offices.

To help you formulate job functions, refer to the Key Action Words below and the sample job descriptions on pages 129 to 138.

---

20 Key Action Words to Describe Job Functions

- Acts
- Recruits
- Processes
- Monitors
- Researches
- Selects
- Prepares

- Issues
- Conducts
- Reports
- Provides
- Decides
- Purchases
- Recommends

- Prices
- Maintains
- Coordinates
- Files
- Orders
- Schedules

Benefits of Using Job Descriptions

Job descriptions, once developed, translate into tremendous managerial benefits for the organization.

Employees know precisely:

- Their duties, responsibilities and limits
- To whom they are responsible
- With whom they are to directly interact
- Whether they are to have direct contact with outside resources or vendors and, if so, which ones
- Criteria on which they can expect to be evaluated.

The written job description is the blueprint that keeps all employees operating within the realm of their own responsibilities. For example: It keeps the accounting people from getting involved in personnel matters, salespeople from getting involved in operations and production people from getting involved in marketing activities.

In a poorly managed company where job responsibilities are not clearly defined, excessive company time is consumed by unguided or misguided effort. Rather than employees effectively planning and managing their time accomplishing specific task/results, they waste time with a lot of "What ifs" and "Yeah, buts" until another day passes with very little accomplished.

Supervisors can use job descriptions to help evaluate performance. Typically, performance reviews are held annually, but why wait an entire year to improve performance when the job description is as close as your file? (Consult Chapter 7 for more information on conducting effective performance appraisals.)

By periodically reviewing the duties and responsibilities of employees, supervisors can effectively praise those behaviors that warrant praise. Duties that are not being handled satisfactorily can be addressed point-by-point and corrected.

Supervisors will save time preparing for employee meetings by using job descriptions as background information. Employees will recognize this document as the ground rules for their employment and will take the meeting seriously.

The written job description settles most questions without dispute because it represents the conditions both management and the employee agreed to at the beginning of their employer/employee relationship.

Ongoing performance management allows the supervisor to anticipate problems and intervene before problems escalate. The supervisor can discuss acceptable performance standards with the employee, develop a plan for making the necessary improvements, and set a time for a follow-up evaluation. It's clean—it's quick—it's effective.

Using Job Descriptions to Improve the Hiring Process

When it is necessary to fill a new position or replace an employee, the job description serves as an important guideline for hiring. By reviewing the current job description, you can first amend it to reflect any new conditions not included in the previous document. Then, you can target your job search toward a person with the exact competencies the job requires.

Too often when a new position is created within a company, an employee who is performing his/her present job duties in a superior manner is promoted into the new position. It's tempting because it's so easy. But the easy way may prove to be the costly way if you place a person in a position for which he or she is not really qualified. You may find yourself with an employee who was happy in the former position and is now disenchanted with the circumstances of the new job.

A well-written job description will help you guard against hiring "the wrong person." The qualifications and the abilities required will be there in writing; and the duties, which are spelled out in detail, will help you ask the right questions as you interview prospective candidates.

Taking the time to find the right person to fill each job is time well-spent. If, after the first round of interviews, you haven't found a suitable candidate, repeat the ad (if that's how you recruit employees), but don't, out of desperation or complacency, change the job description to fit the most willing or available candidate.

If the competency required is not on paper, or is vaguely defined, you are leaving yourself vulnerable to the charmer and the rebound employee.

The charmer is the person with charisma—the kind of person you could just sit and talk with all day—the kind of person you'd like for your friend. In fact, the charmer is such an interesting person, you just know he or she could and would do the job well—not anything like the previous person who gave you so much trouble. Wouldn't it be great to have a person like this in the department? Be careful! Remember, this is an employee you're hiring, not a friend.

The rebound employee possesses all the qualifications the last employee didn't, and those qualities look so appealing! Again, watch out.

Here's an example of how the rebound employee can ruin your best plans: Let's say the last salesman you had, the one you just terminated, met his sales quota most of the time. But every time you tried to find him, it was impossible! Nine times out of ten he wasn't where he said he'd be.

Finally, you terminated him. Now you're interviewing your "best candidate"—the epitome of stability— nice appearance—good family person—likes to be home nights. Red flags! Sure, you want somebody who's stable, but above all you want someone who can sell. Can this person sell? And is he or she willing and able to travel 50 percent of the time?

A detailed list of the competencies a job requires will help keep you on track. When two or more candidates appear equally qualified for the job, the list will provide you with an objective basis for comparing each candidate's qualifications with the job requirements.

So review that job description, keep your eye on the qualifications required, and avoid making big and costly mistakes.

Evaluating Job Descriptions

After reviewing your company's job descriptions as a whole, begin looking for ways to improve their quality and usefulness. Be certain to use the same format for all job descriptions throughout the company so that the same type of information is included in each one. You and others will review the documents more quickly when the format is consistent, and you will avoid the pitfall of omitting important information.

Each job description needs to be broken down by task, both for the benefit of the employee and for the employee's supervisor. The language needs to be precise, leaving no doubt about the work to be done and the level of authority to be exercised.

Job descriptions written to accomplish organizational objectives will help foster a spirit of teamwork, more effective time management and improved productivity. Never should an employee wonder, "Why am I doing this?" because each employee's work is an important link in meeting the company's overall objectives.

Make sure that each employee's job title is correct, non-sexist and consistent with other employees of the same level in other departments. As an example, the use of the terms clerk, technician or analyst should indicate comparable levels throughout the organization. The titles of the supervisors each person reports to must be current, and the employee titles (or groups) to be supervised must be correct.

Each person in an organization deserves to know who his or her immediate supervisor is. And yet, in many companies, employees receive direction from several "bosses." This, of course, causes confusion and may actually result in a lack of accountability to anyone. This lack of direction results in ineffective and unproductive employees. Motivation slips and management may complain, "You just can't get good help anymore."

Titles and employee-group titles rather than individual names will add to the longevity of job descriptions because, in any growing organization, individual names and titles change frequently.

For maximum performance and team effort, communicate clearly what is to be done, who is to do it, who's going to help do it, and to whom each person is accountable. It's vitally important that each person on your payroll knows when to lead and when to follow. It all begins with the job description.

Updating Job Descriptions

How frequently job descriptions should be updated varies from company to company. When job descriptions are used as a performance management tool, they should be updated whenever inaccuracies are noted. But, as a minimum, each employee's job description should be carefully checked for accuracy at the time of each performance appraisal.

If an employee is promoted, demoted, transferred or otherwise moved to a new position, the job description needs to be updated or replaced. If the employee's responsibilities or reporting relationships change, the document should be updated at the time of the change. Also, if a new person is hired to fill an existing position, the job description should be updated before the person is hired to adequately reflect the responsibilities of the job.

The supervisor will then review the document with the employee and have him or her acknowledge and approve the changes by signing or initialing and dating the changes. The employee should be given a copy of the document for reference purposes and encouraged to refer to it periodically.

6 Ways Well-Written Job Descriptions Improve Efficiency and Productivity

1. Well-written job descriptions are task-specific and make clear to each employee every task for which he or she is responsible.

2. Well-written job descriptions include all the tasks that must be performed within an organization. The responsibility for every task is assigned to someone.

3. Well-written job descriptions provide the framework for ongoing performance management and periodic performance reviews.

4. Well-written job descriptions clarify the lines of authority by specifying to whom each employee reports and who reports to the employee.

5. Well-written job descriptions help in recruiting for new positions or in replacing employees who are leaving by listing the tasks that must be performed, the education level required, the skills necessary and the level of competency required. This enables the person conducting the candidate search to specifically target the kind of employee needed and screen applicants accordingly.

6. Well-written job descriptions enable organizations to comply with the Americans with Disabilities Act as well as other state and federal regulations.

Where to Turn for More Information on the ADA

Accessing ADA Sources. A set of seven regional directories on organizations assisting with ADA compliance. Lists local, state and national organizations. Regions include Northeast, Midwest, Far West, Mountain States, South, Southwest, and Mid-Atlantic and Ohio. Contact: Mainstream, Inc., 3 Bethesda Metro Center, Suite 830, Bethesda, MD 20814; (301) 654-2400.

ADA Compliance Advisor. A software program covering up-to-date information from various government agencies. Available on single topics or as a set. Topics include: Equal Employment Opportunity Commission Regulations, Department of Transportation Regulations, Department of Justice Regulations, Department of Justice Regulations (layman's terms), Federal Communications Commission Regulations, and Architectural and Transportation Barriers Compliance Board Regulations. Requires IBM compatible equipment

(DOS 3.0 or higher) and 4 MB of disk space per disk or 11 MB for the set. Contact: Jamestown Area Labor Management Committee, P.O. Box 819, Jamestown, NY 14701-0819.

Project Access Computer Information Center (CIC) Database. A nationwide database assisting employers with ADA compliance. Available 24-hours a day, seven days a week. Compatible with most computer hardware and software; requires modem hook-up. Contact: Project Access Computer Information Center, c/o CEN, 1400 Touhy, Des Plaines, IL 60018; (708) 390-8700.

Sample Job Description #1

Date Written: July 6, 1993

Job Status: Full-time, exempt

Position: Director of Sales

Supervision Received—Reports to: President

Supervision Exercised: Account Managers (salespeople)

Job Summary: Supervises, trains and motivates sales team to meet or exceed annual sales quota. Coordinates activities of Sales Department with Production Manager.

Principal Contacts: President, Account Managers (salespeople), Production Manager and major clients.

Essential Job Functions:

1. Recruits, hires and trains sales staff within established company guidelines.

2. Achieves personal sales/gross profit on orders billed to meet established annual quota.

3. Coordinates and reviews production requirements with Production Manager weekly (more frequently if necessary).

4. Meets weekly with President to review sales activity by individual salespeople.

5. Meets monthly with President to review previous month's sales results and set next month's goals.

6. Drives to each salesperson's territory one day per month and makes full day of sales calls with each one.

7. Conducts 2-day sales orientation meeting with new salespeople quarterly at corporate headquarters.

Non-essential Job Functions:

1. Attends annual trade show in Atlanta.

2. Attends regional trade shows when schedule permits.

Competency Required: Superior sales, motivational and sales management abilities; the perception to recognize potential in other salespeople plus the skills to train and develop those individuals to their maximum potential; ability and stamina required to drive to all sales territories monthly and maintain a rigorous travel schedule.

Education/Experience Required: B.A./B.S. in Business Management, Marketing or related discipline plus five years' sales experience, with at least three years in a management position.

Position Previously Held: Regional Sales Manager.

Career Mobility: Vice President of Sales.

_____   _____

Supervisor   Director of Sales

_____   _____

Date   Date

Sample Job Description #2

Date Written: July 6, 1993

Job Status: Full-time, non-exempt

Position: Secretary

Supervision Received—Reports to: Senior Vice President

Supervision Exercised: None

Job Summary: Handles incoming telephone calls, correspondence, filing, scheduling and other business matters as needed by the Senior Vice President.

Principal Contacts: President, Senior Vice President, Personnel Director and outside contacts of the Senior Vice President.

Essential Job Functions:

1. Provides Senior Vice President with daily agenda of appointments, meetings, travel and other commitments.

2. Takes dictation and generates correspondence, reports and other business writing as required on the word processor.

3. Maintains database of all business contacts.

4. Maintains a flexible schedule to accommodate unexpected or urgent matters.

5. Makes frequent short trips in own car between offices to facilitate work of the sales department.

6. Makes all travel and meeting arrangements for Senior Vice President.

Non-essential Job Functions:

1. Opens and sorts mail as directed.

Competency Required: Excellent communication and telephone skills, organizational abilities and proficiency with latest version of Word Perfect. Ability to handle multiple tasks competently under pressure. Must have own car, valid driver's license and clean driving record.

Education/Experience Required: Associate's degree from an accredited college or university and a minimum of three years' experience in a secretarial position.

_____   _____
Supervisor   Secretary

_____   _____
Date   Date

Sample Job Description #3

Date Written: July 6, 1993

Job Status: Part-time, non-exempt

Position: Bookkeeper

Supervision Received—Reports to: President

Supervision Exercised: None

Job Summary: Responsible for all bookkeeping functions, filing all tax returns, typing of correspondence as needed, assisting with promotional mailings and ordering office supplies as needed.

Principal Contacts: President and Department Heads; clients and office supply vendors.

Essential Job Functions:

1. Maintains accounts payable file, verifies all charges and disburses payments, including all taxes, as they become due.

2. Issues invoices for all products and services, deposits checks, and MasterCard/Visa monies, submits American Express charges for payment daily.

3. Reports status of accounts payable/accounts receivable and other information on the Weekly Barometer Sheet.

4. Maintains the company checking account according to standard bookkeeping/accounting procedures.

5. Issues weekly payroll checks, maintains payroll records and submits all payroll taxes in a timely fashion.

6. Files appropriate forms and submits payments for all taxes as due, including MESC, FUTA and others.

Non-essential Job Functions:

1. Picks up mail at P.O. box daily.

2. Transports bank deposits to the bank each day.

Competency Required: Above-average word processing skills, strong verbal and written communication skills, ability to maintain a full set of books and produce income statements and balance sheets.

Education/Experience Required: Associate's degree in Accounting from an accredited college or university and a minimum of two years' bookkeeping experience. Must be proficient with Peachtree software.

———————————————   ———————————————
Supervisor   Bookkeeper

——————————   ——————————
Date   Date

Sample Job Description #4

Date Written: July 6, 1993

Job Status: Full-time, exempt

Position: Fulfillment Manager

Supervision Received—Reports to: Director of Operations

Supervision Exercised: Inventory Control, Lead Generation Supervisors

Job Summary: To oversee all daily and long-term activities of the fulfillment and lead generation departments.

Principal Contacts: Director of Operations, vendors and suppliers, and other company employees in the fulfillment department.

Essential Job Functions:

1. Recruits and trains fulfillment, inventory, and lead generation department staffs.

2. Monitors and maintains department equipment.

3. Monitors all systems for control weaknesses and possible productivity gains.

4. Prepares annual budget figures for his/her department(s).

5. Conducts fulfillment and lead generation department tours for prospective clients.

6. Schedules and assigns work to those in his/her department to maintain 48-hour delivery promised to customers.

Non-essential Job Functions:

1. Attends annual material handling convention.

Competency Required: Superior organizational and management skills. Proficiency in accounting and scheduling. Careful attention to detail. Must be able to conduct tours through the fulfillment department for prospective clients.

Education/Experience Required: High school diploma plus five years of warehouse experience, with at least three years in a supervisory position. Must be computer literate.

Career Mobility: Director of Operations

_____   _____

Supervisor   Fulfillment Manager

_____   _____

Date   Date

Sample Job Description #5

Date Written: July 6, 1993

Job Status: Full-time, non-exempt

Position: Inventory Control Operator

Supervision Received—Reports to: Inventory Control Manager and Supervisor

Supervision Exercised: Assigned operators

Job Summary: Conducts inventory control on all inbound SKUs, packing materials and catalogs.

Principal Contacts: Other inventory control staff.

Essential Job Functions:

1. Counts inbound items; advises manager/supervisor of any discrepancies.

2. Packages and labels outbound items.

3. Processes returns and exchanges.

4. Prepares outbound package report weekly.

5. Conducts physical inventory every 30 to 45 days and prepares inventory reports.

6. Operates fork lift or other trucks when necessary.

7. Purchases packaging materials from best sources to maintain quality standards and budget criteria.

Non-essential Job Functions:

1. Delivers inventory reports to main office weekly.

Competency Required: Knowledge of inventory management and control; excellent organizational abilities and careful attention to detail. Must be physically capable of operating fork lifts and company trucks on a daily basis.

Education/Experience Required: Two years of ware-house experience. Proficiency in operating computer with one to two years' experience.

Career Mobility: Inventory Control Supervisor

_____   _____
Supervisor   Inventory Control Operator

_____   _____
Date   Date

Sample Job Description Form

Date Written:

Job Status:

Position:

Supervision Received—Reports to:

Supervision Exercised:

Job Summary:

Principal Contacts:

Essential Job Functions:

Non-essential Job Functions:

Competency Required:

Education/Experience Required:

Career Mobility:

Meetings to Attend/Reports to Be Filed:

_____   _____

Supervisor   (Appropriate Job Title)

_____   _____

Date   Date

CHAPTER 7

HOW TO CONDUCT EFFECTIVE PERFORMANCE APPRAISALS

Frequently, the thought of conducting performance appraisals makes employers and supervisors uncomfortable and fearful. Many have unpleasant memories of appraising or being appraised. But, if handled well, performance appraisal can be very rewarding for your company and its workers. Proper performance planning and appraisal boosts morale, increases dedication, and improves productivity.

The purpose of this chapter is to help dispel fears and misconceptions about performance appraisal and to show how to plan and conduct a worker evaluation that will improve performance and increase productivity. A sample performance appraisal work sheet can be found at the end of the chapter.

What Exactly Is a Performance Appraisal?

Many managers and supervisors think of performance appraisals as annual meetings that include standard forms resembling report cards. Effective performance appraisal, however, is an ongoing process conducted for the purpose of improving performance and helping employees work closer to potential. The process can begin as early as the first week on the job, takes place over time and continues as long as the person is employed.

The proper performance appraisal process includes:

- *Performance planning*—A process during which supervisor and worker agree upon performance objectives and expectations to be accomplished within a set time period. The objectives set at this planning meeting serve as the basis of the formal performance appraisal, which follows at some point in the future.

- *Performance monitoring*—A process during which supervisor and worker assess the progress made toward established goals, identify and correct problems, and revise objectives or priorities if necessary.

- *Performance evaluation or appraisal*—A process during which supervisor and worker evaluate accomplishments, set goals for improvement and develop a timetable to reach those goals.

Proper performance planning and monitoring must precede the annual performance evaluation. If you plan for the annual evaluation well before it actually occurs and regularly monitor performance throughout the year, the annual evaluation will prove much more beneficial and productive.

What's the Purpose of a Performance Appraisal?

Corporations and other organizations use performance appraisals for many reasons:

- To establish goals and objectives with individuals

- To inform people of raises and promotions

- To assess the company's potential personnel needs.

Performance appraisals provide a way for managers and supervisors to regularly communicate their expectations to employees and to monitor employees' performance. Because a supervisor's schedule is often hectic and stressful, the need for regular performance planning and monitoring is important. Regular performance appraisals allow managers and workers to communicate more frequently and help to alleviate pressure that can mount between annual evaluations.

Managers and supervisors are not the only ones with much to gain from performance planning and monitoring. Workers benefit from knowing exactly what is expected of them by their supervisors as well as what they must do to achieve their goals. Perhaps most important, they realize that they will be held accountable for their performance.

In addition to these benefits, performance planning and monitoring also help satisfy workers' needs for recognition by rewarding positive performance. Performance appraisal gives people an opportunity to plan for and discuss their own career growth. Accurate and timely feedback will inform them of their strengths and weaknesses and help them work closer to their potential.

How to Conduct a Performance Appraisal

As mentioned earlier, the overall performance appraisal process involves:

- Performance planning

- Performance monitoring

- Performance appraisal.

Before conducting an actual performance evaluation, you must have a thorough understanding of performance planning and performance monitoring.

Performance Planning

Performance planning is a two-way communication process between employee and supervisor during which performance goals and objectives are set for a specific time period. Effective performance planning requires involvement, integration and importance.

Involvement

Involvement is the act of encouraging an individual to set attainable goals and actively participate in the goal-setting. You can become involved by:

- Meeting with the individual to set goals and objectives

- Encouraging expression of ideas and opinions while setting goals

- Adding your input when establishing performance objectives

- Verifying that the individual understands the goals and is committed to reaching them.

Integration

Integration is the act of ensuring that a person's goals support the organization and vice versa. You can help the integration process by:

- Communicating organizational goals

- Discussing how individual goals relate to organizational goals

- Telling the individual how his or her achievements have helped attain organizational goals

- Emphasizing the importance of mutual goals between co-workers.

Importance

It is vital that you communicate the importance of goals and establish priorities for achieving those goals. You can communicate the importance of goal setting by:

- Helping the individual prioritize his or her goals

- Providing rationale for the order of priorities

- Ensuring that the individual recognizes and agrees with the prioritized goals

- Communicating the importance of individual goals in relation to overall organizational goals.

Following is an example inappropriate performance planning:

Tom, Manager: Hi, Pete. I've taken a few minutes to draft a set of goals and objectives for you. Take a look at them when you have a chance.

Pete: Oh, I didn't realize it was time for goals to be submitted.

Tom: That's OK. I have a pretty good idea of your responsibilities for the next few months, and I got them all ready for you.

Pete: Well, I would like to . . .

Tom: They're on your desk. Oh, by the way, they aren't in any special order. I just jotted them down as they came to mind. See you later.

Now look at an example of appropriate performance planning:

Tom, Manager: Pete, thanks for taking time out of your schedule to meet today. I want to work together on setting some performance goals and objectives. I'd also like to review your goals from last quarter. I must say, after looking them over, you've done very well. Your increased sales have helped the department and the company achieve new sales records.

Pete: Thanks, Tom. I worked hard on developing a wider customer base and developing several outlying areas.

Tom: Your efforts paid off! Now, since we spoke last week, have you developed a tentative list of goals and objectives for this quarter?

Pete: Yes, I believe my goals are realistic and attainable, based on my past achievements.

Tom: Let's first discuss your goals and objectives from last quarter, then we'll move on to those you've prepared for next quarter.

As you can see from the above scenarios, performance planning is a very important element of the appraisal process. The first situation was ineffective because it was unplanned and handled as though it was of little or no importance. In the second scenario, however, the importance of goal setting is stressed. Proper performance planning gives you a solid foundation on which to build the second phase of the performance appraisal process—performance monitoring.

Performance Monitoring

Performance monitoring is also a two-way communication process. It includes evaluating the progress to date toward achieving previously established goals, identifying areas that need further attention and, if necessary, rearranging priorities. Proper performance monitoring requires observation, feedback and coaching.

Observation

Observation allows you to collect information that will help you assess a person's progress toward achieving his or her goals. You can practice observation by:

- Discreetly viewing an individual's performance in different situations

- Identifying problems before they affect outcomes

- Collecting performance information throughout the entire performance period

- Keeping accurate written records of performance data.

Feedback

Regular feedback is essential to keeping the lines of communication open. You can provide feedback by:

- Discussing progress and problems regularly

- Rewarding positive performance as it occurs

- Confronting performance problems immediately

- Maintaining current performance objectives and priorities.

Coaching

A supervisor should always be more of a coach than an evaluator. Coaching involves guiding, instructing and helping people to meet performance goals. You can act as a coach by:

- Noticing and removing performance barriers

- Suggesting ways to work more effectively

- Using performance difficulties as opportunities to develop new skills

- Providing support and guidance.

Following is an example of inappropriate performance monitoring:

Sue, Manager: Kate, I'd like to see you in my office right away, please.

Kate: Is something wrong?

Sue: Yes, I've been reviewing last month's production schedule. Your productivity decreased by 12 percent and now we're having trouble filling orders.

Kate: I was sick for a few days, but I never realized there was a problem.

Sue: Well, there is a problem. You need to increase your productivity and make up for some of that lost time. I expect a big improvement this month.

Now look at an example of appropriate performance monitoring:

Sue, Manager: Kate, thanks for meeting with me this afternoon. Are you feeling better?

Kate: Yes, I'm feeling much better, thank you.

Sue: We missed you last week—you are a valuable member of our team. There is something I would like to talk about with you. I have noticed recently that your productivity has been gradually decreasing. You're normally much more productive at work. Is there anything wrong?

Kate: Yes, I've been feeling pressured under our new supervisor. She pushes me all the time, and I get nervous and make mistakes.

Sue: Give me an example of what you mean. (Waits for Kate to respond, then continues.) Thanks for telling me. I didn't realize there was a problem. Let me see what I can do about the situation. As I said, you work very hard, and you do quality work. Let's meet again Friday at this same time to discuss whether the situation has improved.

In the first example, Sue was far too curt and failed to consider the special circumstances affecting Kate's productivity. In the second example, Sue was pleasant, asked open-ended questions and listened to what Kate had to say about her productivity.

Careful performance planning and performance monitoring will provide the foundation for a successful performance appraisal.

Performance Appraisal

The annual performance evaluation should be carefully planned and thoughtfully considered. Many workers dread and fear their performance evaluation but, with careful preparation, you can alleviate their fears and make the meeting productive and beneficial for both parties. Follow the steps listed below when preparing for the performance appraisal.

Step 1: Schedule wisely.

• Decide when the evaluation will take place.

Schedule the appraisal during a time when it will not be interrupted and when you and the employee can devote full attention to the meeting. Also, make sure you have allotted enough time for the meeting. It will take at least one to one-and-a-half hours. After you have decided on a time, notify the individual well in advance, and do not change the appointment unless it is absolutely necessary.

• Decide where the evaluation will take place.

The evaluation setting should be very private; no one should be able to overhear your conversation. Conduct the meeting in a place where you can sit face-to-face without a desk or table between you. If you need to sit at a table to write, sit on the same side of the table. Some workers may feel uncomfortable being evaluated in your office. If necessary, conduct the meeting in their office or in a "neutral" conference room.

Step 2: Review carefully.

• Collect information.

If possible, review the individual's previous appraisal and note whether earlier goals were achieved. Also, read his or her job description. The description should outline principal duties and responsibilities, which will allow you to assess whether the job is getting done. If applicable, it may also be helpful to go over production or sales reports. These will give you a quantitative picture of the person's performance.

- Remain objective.

  Remember to be fair and objective. It is not fair to the person to assess only his or her performance over the past week. This is where regular feedback and daily communication play an important role. If you are meeting briefly and regularly with the individual, you will both be attuned to his or her progress, and this will help you as you prepare for the annual evaluation.

  As you prepare what you are going to address in the appraisal, remember to concentrate on the significant matters. Supervisors who note only the minute details of the job and overlook the important aspects will arouse resentment rather than boost morale or improve productivity.

- Seek additional opinions.

  Seeking the opinions of other managers or supervisors who have worked with the person to be evaluated will give you another view and may help to affirm your judgment. Requesting others' opinions is especially helpful if the person you are evaluating has worked with you for only a short time. You may want to prepare your evaluation and then review it with the individual's former supervisor.

  If you do seek additional opinions, remember to carefully weigh everything that is said and consider any biases that the evaluator may have toward the person. Never accept personality or character evaluations; performance is the only criteria you should consider.

- Complete the appraisal form.

  Whether your company or organization has a standard appraisal form or you design one for your own use, it is important to use some type of measuring device. A form will help you to be more objective and will serve as a standard for the evaluation. Think of the form as the catalyst to your discussion with the employee; it should stimulate the worker to move closer to his or her potential.

  Many managers think of the appraisal form as a list of general characteristics to be evaluated on a scale from "poor" to "excellent." However, a completed appraisal form must be more than a series of check marks. Appraisal forms must be tailored to the company, the work force, and the organization's goals. If necessary, one basic form can usually be customized to the needs of several departments within the company. If you are designing a form, remember to:

  - Write in terms that people can understand

  - Request subjective and objective information

  - Allow adequate space for comments

  - Provide a specific place where both the employee and the appraiser can sign the form

  - Allow several co-workers to critique the form and offer input before you implement it.

  Although performance appraisal is much more than completing the appraisal form, documentation is very important. As you will see in the upcoming section, "Legal Aspects of Performance Appraisals," thorough documentation can serve as important evidence if there is a dispute requiring a court decision. It is vital that you keep accurate evaluation records. A sample appraisal form is included at the end of this report to help you in preparing your own appraisal form.

Step 3: Request a self-appraisal.

Self-appraisals can provide valuable insight about the individual and his or her job situation; however, an individual's self-evaluation may be in sharp contrast to your appraisal. For example, Bill may feel he is conscientious and thorough. Yet you have observed several instances where his hasty inspections have compromised your department's excellent reputation. When you present your evaluation, Bill could become angry and defensive—he may even accuse you of slander. Because of this, it is a good idea to consult your labor attorney before you decide to implement self-appraisals. Learn about the possible legal ramifications of self-appraisal before deciding whether to include this in your appraisal procedure.

If you choose to request self-appraisals, do not ask people to evaluate their character; this will only encourage defensiveness. Confine your questions to job performance issues. Have they reached their goals? Were the goals and objectives reasonable? How are they getting along with their co-workers?

It would not be fair to confront the individual on the day of the annual evaluation and ask him or her to do a self-appraisal. You should allow at least a week for people to prepare and contemplate their responses. Suggest that the individual read his or her previous appraisal and job description so that you are both well-prepared for the meeting. Also, tell him or her the purpose of the appraisal meeting; this may increase honesty and frankness in the self-appraisal. Be careful to communicate that you are interested in the individual's opinions and feedback, even if they are negative. Assure the employee that your discussion will be positive and helpful.

Step 4: Prepare for the evaluation.

After you have collected the background information and set a meeting time, you will need to prepare the information that you intend to use in the evaluation. As you prepare, remember to limit your meeting objectives and the topics you want to discuss. Choose to discuss only important matters that will make a difference in the person's work and attitude.

If you think of several areas where the individual could improve, mention only the three or four most important ones. Do not overburden the worker by asking him or her to improve in 15 different ways. Encourage gradual improvement. Also, after you note the areas that need improvement, be prepared to suggest training or ways in which he or she can address these problems. Be specific. Work together to set measurable goals for the individual and a timetable for achieving them.

Finally, draw up an agenda for your meeting. The following is an example of an agenda:

1. Supervisor opens the meeting by stating objectives. He or she sets a tone of openness and free discussion.

2. Individual presents self-appraisal.

3. Supervisor responds to worker's remarks and presents own appraisal.

4. Both parties examine possible causes for any problems.

5. Both set objectives and outline plan, including specific dates, for achieving objectives. Set a tentative date for the next review.

6. Supervisor summarizes main points of the evaluation.

Although the agenda may appear rigid, the meeting itself should be pleasant and conversational. The agenda is simply there to guide the flow and direction of the meeting.

Step 5: Conduct the performance appraisal.

The annual evaluation meeting has three main objectives:

*   To assess performance since the last review and determine what can be done to improve it

*   To learn what motivates each individual and how s/he perceives her/his own performance

*   To set specific goals and objectives for future performance.

At the start of the meeting, establish good rapport and relieve the individual's nervousness. Remember that fear of embarrassment or criticism and anticipation of how this meeting may affect a raise or a promotion are weighing heavily on the person's mind. Acknowledge the nervousness, stating that it is natural, and reassure the person that the meeting will be positive and profitable.

Keep the following advice in mind as you conduct the rest of the evaluation:

• Ask open-ended questions.

There are several advantages to asking open-ended questions and allowing the worker to speak first. If you, as an authority figure, give your opinion first, the individual may be reluctant to give his or her true opinion(s). Out of fear or lack of confidence, he or she may verbally concede, but not necessarily agree with, all of your points. Allowing workers to speak first helps you to understand their perspectives and perceptions.

Your workers' input will be especially important as you proceed together to set goals for future performance. You must be able to incorporate their input when developing these goals. If their input is not considered, employees may not buy into performance goals. Also, an individual's willingness to speak provides valuable insight about his or her self-concept and attitudes toward work. This may help you in communicating negative information and in coaching the person on to greater achievements.

As the individual is speaking, listen carefully. Try not to think about what your responses will be or make mental notes, but concentrate totally on what he or she is saying. Here are some suggestions to help you listen skillfully:

• Listen for emotional messages as well as spoken messages. Pay attention to non-verbal cues, and respond when appropriate.

• Maintain good eye contact while the other person is speaking.

- Give occasional feedback in the form of nodding or comments, such as, "I agree" or "Exactly" or "Go on."

- If you are unsure of what is being said, interrupt gently so you can make sure. Never assume that you know what a person is saying. If you are uncertain of a person's meaning, ask a question like, "It seems to me that you are saying. . ." or "Have I understood you correctly?" or "Tell me what you mean by that."

- Present your own appraisal.

  If you have prepared properly for your annual meeting, presenting your own appraisal should not be

difficult. As you speak to the worker, keep in mind two things: what you say and how you say it.

What You Say

- Emphasize the positive aspects and be specific. Dwell on each point long enough for the person to take pride in what he or she has done well.

- Be direct without being critical when addressing areas that need improvement. Concentrate on only the few most important areas.

- Communicate observations rather than conclusions. For example: If Jane has missed several deadlines in the past few weeks, tell her that you noticed projects have been late and ask if there is a problem. Do not communicate that Jane is lazy, doesn't care or is not concentrating on her work.

- Convey your appreciation for the individual's hard work and give the person an opportunity to talk about areas where he or she performs well.

- Avoid giving a "laundry list" of trivial problems.

- Ask open-ended questions throughout your meeting, such as, "What do you think of the new computer system?" or "What part of your work do you enjoy most?" These questions require more than a yes or no answer and will encourage the individual to share his or her opinion.

How You Say It

- Be sensitive to a person's fears and apprehensions. Speak in a pleasing tone and accentuate the positive. Be reassuring.

- Avoid putting the individual on the defensive.

- Do not attack or even discuss a person's character.

- Avoid leading questions like, "Do you feel, like most people, that you are overworked?" or "You didn't reach your sales goals last month, did you?" This type of question usually elicits a biased response.

- Support your information with specific examples.

- Confine your discussion to job performance, relationships with co-workers and accomplishments since the last performance review.

- State your thoughts clearly in a straightforward manner.

- Communicate negative information properly.

  There are times when managers and supervisors must communicate negative aspects of a person's performance. Although it is important to emphasize the positive, sometimes negative feedback is unavoidable. If you are placed in this difficult situation, remember the following:

  - *Be open and honest*—It is best to convey negative information early, but not in the very beginning of the evaluation. Put the person at ease first and give some reassurances before moving into the negative comments. This will "clear the air" and allow you to talk freely about possible solutions.

- *Be specific*—Tell the individual exactly what he or she did or did not do and give specific examples of the behavior. Be brief and do not dwell on the failure(s).

- *Be helpful*—Offer solutions and encourage the worker to provide possible solutions. Give several alternative courses of action that may help to improve the negative performance.

- *Be encouraging*—Communicate that you are confident in the person's ability to improve if he or she puts forth good effort.

- *Be supportive*—Ask how you can help to solve the problem. Be willing to provide assistance in any way you can, but be careful to communicate that the person is ultimately responsible for correcting the problem.

- Review expectations and set goals.

If, after your discussion, you have identified several areas for improvement, review your basic expectations with the individual. Poor performance may result if the person does not fully understand what is expected.

Work together to establish a plan of action with dates for accomplishment. Help the person set goals; provide guidance in establishing objectives and time limits. Encourage people to "lead" themselves and offer to help in the process. Often people will set unattainable goals in an effort to impress their manager or supervisor. If you sense this is a problem, gently caution the individual and encourage him or her to set reasonable goals.

If an individual has maintained positive performance, compliment the achievements and encourage him or her to set challenging goals that will expand present abilities. If the person's performance indicates that a promotion may be forthcoming, assist in developing personal growth objectives so that he or she can prepare for the next step.

A note of caution: If a promotion or raise are only possibilities, do not give the individual false hopes. Too many managers have mentioned a possible promotion or pay raise and then had to relay bad news when the promotion or raise did not occur. Make sure your information is absolutely correct before you tell the individual of a promotion or raise, and never say anything that sets up strong expectations or implies a guarantee.

- Close the meeting on a positive note.

  End your meeting on a good note. Mention positive performance again and offer praise for accomplishments. Thank the worker for valuable input and be encouraging as he or she prepares to face new challenges.

  Before you close the meeting, summarize your entire discussion, including the goals and the date of your next meeting to review progress. You should have in your hands two documents: your written evaluation and a copy of the future action plan. (If developed during the meeting, the action plan should be typed and delivered to the employee within a day or two.)

- Document each appraisal meeting.

   It is imperative that you document each appraisal meeting. Your documentation should include the following:

   - A specific listing of the successes and problems of the performance period

   - A careful record of any disagreements between you and the worker

   - A copy of the action plan that you have agreed upon

   - Signatures of both parties to show that the performance appraisal meeting did occur.

   Documentation is very important. Written reports of performance evaluations can have great legal significance if an individual should ever bring litigation against the company. A general form with some check marks will not stand up in court. The documentation must be specific and must be signed by both parties.

Legal Aspects of Performance Appraisals

Because performance appraisal methods are often subjective, many performance decisions, including promotions and raises, are based on arbitrary judgment and personal feelings rather than facts. This has led to numerous court cases; often, the court rules in favor of the employee. In order to protect yourself and your company, you must understand the legal ramifications of ineffective and illegal performance appraisals.

The Equal Employment Opportunity Commission (EEOC) has established the following performance appraisal guidelines for employers:

- Companies cannot use any selection procedure that discriminates against a protected group, which includes but is not limited to the handicapped, women, the elderly and racial minorities.

- The company will be found guilty if the selection procedure discriminates against a disproportionate number of people in a certain group. The company does not have to intend to discriminate.

- These rules apply to anything that may influence an employment decision.

The practices recommended in this chapter will help you conduct performance appraisals that are proper and legal. Use the following guidelines to ensure that your company's practices are acceptable:

- Conduct written appraisals and always base them on a specific job description.

- Do not appraise an individual if you are unfamiliar with his or her job requirements.

- Never evaluate someone's personality or character.

- Never comment on race, creed, color, sex or handicap.

- Do not make accusatory remarks unless you can prove that the information is correct.

- Base your appraisal on several observations; do not write a negative appraisal after an uncharacteristic mistake.

- Show the appraisal to the individual and ask him or her to sign it. If the person does not agree with the evaluation, provide a place for him or her to sign in disagreement. Also, allow employees to appeal if they feel they were evaluated unfairly.

- Keep written documentation of the negative and/or positive reasons for each employment decision.

- Ensure the privacy of appraisal records.

The Importance of Effective Performance Appraisal

Although it is easy to overlook or ignore the need for performance evaluations, they are a vital part of today's business world. An individual's positive performance may not continue unless it is acknowledged; negative performance may continue until the problem is solved.

Effective performance appraisal is difficult. It requires skill, time and commitment. If you make a concentrated effort, however, to plan, monitor and evaluate performance regularly, your investment will pay big dividends in the form of happy, productive employees.

Additional information on performance appraisal may be found in *Behavioral Supervision: Practical Ways to Change Unsatisfactory Behavior and Increase Productivity* by Les Donaldson (Reading, MA: Addison-Wesley, 1980) and *Coaching for Improved Work Performance* by Ferdinand F. Fournies (New York: Van Nostrand Reinhold, 1978).

Name:_____

Title:_____

ABC Service Company
Sample Performance Appraisal

1 - Needs Improvement   **2 - Meets Expectations**
3 - Significant Strength   **N - Not Applicable**

Job Performance Overall Rating _____

1. **Quality**—completes tasks accurately and neatly

    _____

2. **Timeliness**—eliminates unnecessary steps to meet
    deadlines   _____

3. **Flexibility**—adapts to changes; maintains composure and
    adjusts pace to the urgency of a situation_____

4. **Organization**—plans and develops accurate timetables
    and priorities   _____

5. **Cost Awareness**—works within budget; chooses cost-
    effective work methods   _____

6. **Problem-solving**—recognizes problems quickly; recom-
    mends effective solutions   _____

Interpersonal Skills

1. **Oral Communication**—speaks effectively with clients
    and co-workers   _____

2. **Written Communication**—produces concise and read-
    able memos, reports and letters   _____

3. **Teamwork**—works effectively in a team situation

    _____

4. **Leadership**—gives clear direction and listens to
    co-workers   _____

Attitude

1. **Initiative**—a self-starter; able to work without constant supervision   _____

2. **Responsibility**—understands duties; accepts responsibility for work   _____

3. **Punctuality**—arrives on time and does not leave early

                                                        _____

4. **Loyalty**—supports and follows company policies and guidelines   _____

5. **Development**—works to improve job performance through training, reading and continuous learning

                                                        _____

The candidate's primary strengths: _____

_____

The candidate's areas for improvement: _____

_____

The strategies we agreed upon for improvement: _____

_____

Goals, objectives and dates for next performance period:

_____

Employee Comments

_____   I agree with this evaluation.

_____   I agree with this evaluation except in the areas noted below.

_____   I disagree with this evaluation for the reasons noted below.

Comments:_____

Signatures

Employee_____Date _____

Reviewer _____Date _____

CHAPTER 8

HOW TO WRITE OR UPDATE YOUR EMPLOYEE MANUAL

Initially, a company policy manual may not appear to be a necessity. But if you want your business to thrive rather than just survive, you'll want to develop and implement policies that are legally sound and practical from a management perspective. A successful business owner or personnel executive recognizes:

- The need for consistent decision-making

- The inefficiency of making on-the-spot decisions repeatedly on similar issues

- The necessity of having written policies in place to ensure the growth and survival of the business

- The added risk of employee litigation for companies operating without a legally sound policy manual.

Some executives like the feeling of importance they enjoy when called upon to make every decision. But this is a risky and inefficient way to manage a business. Your employees will be more secure—and so will your business—when you put your personnel policies in writing.

The purpose of this chapter is to provide basic guidelines you'll need to:

- Write your own personnel manual

- Evaluate a proposal from an outside source offering to write the manual for you

- Critique the manual while it's in progress.

Your policy manual may be considered legally binding in the event of a dispute or an unfair employment practice claim. Therefore, consulting a lawyer who specializes in the field of labor relations is a must before issuing a personnel policy manual to employees. A labor attorney will advise you of the latest legal opinions on issues such as equal opportunity regulations, at-will employment, pregnancy and disability leave, and federal and state regulations. A labor relations attorney will also caution you about the use of certain words and phrases that could weaken your position in the courtroom.

Federal and state government regulations continually change and frequently expand. Consult the listing of federal laws at the end of this chapter.

The Types of Personnel Manuals

Organizations use many different types of manuals and names for those manuals. Terminology is not always consistent. The following definitions may help you determine the contents of the manual you are about to write:

- *Employee manual*—Addresses questions employees frequently ask about work hours, overtime, grievance procedures, leaves of absence and other personnel issues that may have legal implications for the employer.

- *Benefits handbook*—Describes the various benefits employees may select under a cafeteria plan or are entitled to under certain conditions. Holiday pay, health insurance, child care provisions and tuition reimbursement are topics typically included in a benefits handbook.

- *Policy manual*—Includes statements on how the organization consistently deals with specific situations, such as cash shortages, disciplinary matters and sexual harassment.

- *Operations manual*—A complete written description of every facet of an organization's operating policies, procedures, job descriptions, and reporting relationships; usually includes an organization chart and copies of forms used throughout the company.

- *Procedures manual*—Explains step-by-step how to perform specific procedures, such as how to clean a piece of equipment, how to take inventory on the last day of the month, or how to reconcile a bank statement with the general ledger.

Any of the manuals described above, except the operations manual, may be combined with another. In this chapter, we will combine the employee and policy manuals and sections of the benefits manual. Because health insurance coverage and providers change frequently, we recommend that you furnish information directly from the health care administrator or address insurance in a separate document.

What Is the Difference Between Policies and Procedures?

The phrase "policies and procedures" frequently arises in any discussion about manuals. Note the difference in the word definitions when writing your manual:

- A *policy* tells what and/or why. For example: "All company vehicles are to be washed and serviced weekly at the company service garage."

- A *procedure* is a step-by-step description of how. For example: "All route drivers are to bring their company vehicles to the service garage by 3:00 p.m. on Fridays. The vehicles should be parked in the adjoining lot with keys in the ignition. The vehicle maintenance workers will then wash the exteriors of the trucks and inside the trailers using hot water and Truck E-Z Clean dispensed at one part per 10 through the high-power hoses provided for that purpose. Drivers will pick up the keys to their vehicles between 6:30 and 7:00 a.m. on Mondays at the service garage main service counter."

What Are the Benefits of a Well-Written Employee Manual?

Having an up-to-date employee manual will:

- Make a positive statement to prospective employees
- Boost morale and add to the security of your current staff
- Ensure that policies are upheld consistently and fairly
- Communicate to your work force that you take your management responsibilities seriously.

Your employee policy manual also provides an opportunity to convey to your employees, in writing, important information regarding:

- Your business objectives
- Company history
- Company philosophy
- Goals and aspirations of your organization.

A well-written employee policy manual—once approved by your labor attorney—will add to the security of your organization and the effectiveness of your management team by:

- Minimizing the risk of employee litigation

- Establishing and defining legally defensible management practices

- Providing written documentation for supervisor support and authoritative reference for workers at all levels

- Informing employees before rather than after the fact of company policies on bereavement, jury duty, safety, dress code, and other pertinent issues.

Company Orientation for New Employees

Workers are most "teachable" during their first few days on the job. This is an ideal time to communicate information they will need to know, such as:

- *Work permits and deviation of hours*—Federal law requires any employee under 18 years of age who has not graduated from high school to apply for a work permit. Many states do not allow hiring people under age 16. Employees under 18 years of age must have a current deviation of hours form and a work permit on file to work past 10:00 p.m.

- *Social security number*—Employees must have a social security number on file at the personnel office before starting work.

- *Immigration Reform and Control Act (1986)*—This act requires every company, regardless of size, to complete an official form approved by the Attorney General for every immigrant it recruits, refers for a fee, or hires.

- *Physical examinations*—Establish your right to conduct physical exams, including drug testing, at company expense both before and after hiring a person. The Americans With Disabilities Act, enacted in July of 1992, states that employers may require physical exams only after a bonafide job offer has been made to prospective employees.

- *Alcohol*—Alcohol use in the work place is an expensive problem. Experts estimate that approximately 45 percent of industrial injuries and fatalities can be linked to alcohol abuse. Most employers enact policies prohibiting inebriation and the use of alcohol while working or while on company premises.

- *Drug testing*—Many employers test job applicants for drug use and almost all have adopted explicit rules and policies regarding drug use on the job. Unfortunately, there is no legal definition of drug intoxication. Employers must be aware of employees' right to privacy and possible claims of defamation, negligence and dismissal without cause.

  A strong anti-drug policy that is enforced by management conveys to your employees the seriousness of this issue. A statement proclaiming your right to search lockers, cars, lunch boxes, and other places under appropriate circumstances may deter drug and alcohol use and curtail legal problems should it become necessary to conduct such a search. Employees will be less likely to pursue a charge of violation of privacy if you have a written policy in effect.

  Some organizations engage employee assistance programs to help workers with substance abuse problems. These organizations serve as a buffer between the employer and the problem employee and put the responsibility for correcting the problem on the employee.

- *Pre-employment driving record investigation*—Your company could be accused of negligent practices if you fail to check the driving record of an employee who is later involved in an accident while operating a company vehicle. Review your company's liability policy in conjunction with your decision to check or not check driving records.

- *Pre-employment credit investigation*—Now that polygraph testing is no longer legal, companies are turning to credit screening as an alternative evaluation tool. Consult your labor attorney on whether or not you must receive written authorization from the prospective employee before conducting a credit check.

Working Regulations at Your Company

- *Attendance*—Communicate the importance of each person being on the job at the appointed time for the entire scheduled period. State what you expect the employee to do if he/she is unable to be at work at the appointed time due to illness or emergency. Also, indicate what action will be taken if absences are excessive.

- *Sign-in system*—Explain how your sign-in system or time clock correlates to your payroll process. Employees who falsify work records, mark the time card of another employee, or consistently neglect to complete individual time records may be disciplined up to and including termination for repeated violations.

- *Employee status (or classification)*—When defining
  employee classifications, avoid using the word "per-
  manent" or any other word that may be construed as
  guaranteed employment or an employment contract.
  The word "regular" is a better choice.

  You may also want to classify employees as either
  exempt or nonexempt. Exempt employees are those
  who are not eligible for overtime compensation.
  Your definition of each classification will affect
  employee benefits, work hours and perhaps even
  severance pay. Rely on the advice of your labor
  attorney for classifications in your state and in your
  particular business.

- *Service with the company*—This too may affect
  claims on benefits, severance and vacation pay so
  you need to be very precise in the way you define
  the various terms describing service with the company. Does service pertain to regular full-time
  employment only, or continuous employment
  whether full-time or part-time?

- *Workweek*—Define the beginning day and time of
  each workweek for accurate calculation of pay periods and overtime.

- *Cash control policy*—If your business has employees who handle cash transactions, establish policies
  on daily cash reconciliation, overages and shortages,
  and indicate who is authorized to handle such transactions.

- *Employee discounts*—If employees are entitled to
  discounts on food, merchandise or services, carefully outline any special conditions.

- *Lunch and rest periods*—All hourly employees
  working eight hours or more in a work day are

allowed a paid 15-minute rest period in each half of their regular shift and an unpaid lunch hour of 30 or 60 minutes. Salaried employees may or may not get rest periods; they do, of course, get lunch periods.

If you are paying for rest periods, you have the right to limit what employees may do during this time. For example: You may state that employees are not allowed to leave the premises.

- *Change of address, marital status or dependents*— The ultimate decision on employee classification is a management decision based on definitions already in place. Any changes in employee classification should be documented in the employee's personal file with a copy given to the employee. Employees must advise their supervisors and the payroll depart-ment of changes in address, telephone number, num-ber of dependents, marital status as well as other changes in employee classification they believe are warranted.

- *Smokeless environment*—Smoking may be prohibit-ed entirely or limited to designated areas.

Explaining Your Company's Wages and Work Practices

State that your organization is in compliance with applicable laws prohibiting discrimination in employ-ment based on race, color, religion, national origin, age, sex, marital status, veteran status, handicap, or other pro-tected characteristics.

- *Bonding of employees*—State that all employees handling cash will be bonded if that is a true statement.

- *Overtime*—Be very specific about what constitutes overtime. Is it work time exceeding eight hours a

*"Now hold on, Mike. You're talking about embezzlement!
And unless I'm very mistaken, that's strictly prohibited in the
company's employee handbook!"*

day or time worked in addition to a regular 40-hour
workweek? Will you pay time-and-a-half for hourly
employees only?

Under what conditions, if any, will you pay double
time? Must all overtime be authorized in advance
by the employee's supervisor? How will you distribute overtime? When asked to work overtime,
must scheduled employees do so?

*   *Employment-at-will*—State that both the employee
    and the company have the right to terminate at-will
    employment at any time. Then ask your labor attor-
    ney to be certain you haven't said anything in your
    manual that negates that statement.

- *Outside employment*—Establish a policy on outside employment for employees who may choose to work a second job. Do you wish to specify that any outside employment must be in a non-competing business?

- *Employment of relatives*—Under what conditions, if any, will you employ relatives? Stipulations such as, "An employee's superior should not be a relative," or, "Relatives must work in different departments" are common.

- *Emergency shutdowns*—When employees report for work as scheduled and for unforeseen reasons have to be sent home before the completion of their shift, will you pay a minimum two hour "reporting pay" or actual hours worked only? Reserve the right to ask people to do other work to qualify for reporting pay; those who refuse may forfeit pay.

  If, due to weather or other conditions, employees are advised of a shutdown via telephone or radio prior to reporting for work, you may elect to pay no compensation for that day.

- *Work at home*—Establish a policy that all work be performed on company premises or at designated job sites and within scheduled working hours, unless approved in advance under special circumstances.

- *Wages*—Include a statement about your policy of reviewing hourly rates and benefits annually.

- *Payroll checks*—Include information regarding:

  - Payroll period

  - Distribution of checks–when–where–by whom?

  - How a check is to be picked up/delivered if the employee is absent or not scheduled to work on payday

- *Lost paychecks*—State clearly the procedure employees should follow if they lose their paychecks.

- *Payroll deductions*—Explain the taxes and other deductions affecting payroll checks. Be sure to note that the company pays matching amounts for FICA to help fund workers' eventual retirement income.

  Remind employees of their responsibility to keep the payroll department informed of any changes in their marital status, tax deductions and insurance dependency status.

- *Expense reimbursement*—List expenses you will reimburse and under what conditions. If different rules apply to the salespeople or route drivers, provide the necessary information to those individuals only.

- *Severance pay*—Base severance pay on seniority, and list the amount you will grant for years worked. You are not obligated to pay severance pay by law. If you do choose to pay severance pay, you have no obligation to pay employees who are released for reasons covered under your dismissal policy or those who leave voluntarily to work for someone else. State laws vary on payment of accrued vacation time; universally, employees believe they deserve it regardless of the law. Discuss this with your labor attorney and follow his/her advice.

Spelling Out Benefits

Include an opening paragraph about how pleased you are to provide health insurance and other benefits for your employees. List, by employee classification, employees who qualify for health care coverage and whether employees may purchase health care insurance for their immediate family members at the group rate. Decide whether employees who choose not to be insured under the plan you offer will be compensated in part or in full.

Tell employees where they may find complete information about their coverage, claim forms and answers to their questions. State that you have a right to modify, suspend, terminate or cancel the plan without notice when, in the opinion of management, circumstances require it.

- *Medical leaves*—State how medical leaves are granted and what type of documentation is required. List any limitations on other benefits, such as holiday pay, when an employee is on medical leave.

- *Temporary extension of health coverage*—If your company employs twenty or more people, mention that employees who leave the company for any reason (including those who have been laid off or terminated) and have been covered by health benefits have the right to temporarily continue group health insurance coverage on your policy. Said employees must pay for the full cost of such benefits (Consolidated Omnibus Budget Reconciliation Act of 1985, "COBRA").

- *Disability benefits*—Provide information about your disability insurance and address the specifics of your coverage, including eligibility, documentation required, restrictions and other pertinent details.

- *Holidays*—List all paid holidays. List job classifications that are eligible for holiday pay and the length of employment required to qualify. Also, state payment compensation policy for holidays that fall within an employee's vacation or during a leave of absence.

Some companies award additional floating holidays or personal days for employees who have been with the company for a specified period of time. If you do not want floating holidays to carry over to the next year and/or do not want them to be payable upon termination if not taken, state the policy you will follow.

If you provide additional holidays for certain employee classifications, list in your manual only those holidays that are paid for all classifications.

* *Vacations*—List employee classifications that will qualify for vacation pay and under what conditions. For example: "All regular full-time employees who have worked one year, or 2,000 hours, during the preceding vacation year are eligible for vacation with pay according to the schedule below."

When listing the vacation pay schedule, state five days vacation pay, rather than one week, which could be construed as seven days vacation pay. If employees will be paid according to their regular hourly rate at the time the vacation pay is disbursed rather than at their average weekly wage over the past year, state that in your manual.

What is the minimum vacation time you will allow employees to take? May employees accumulate vacation time from year to year? What procedure should employees follow when requesting vacation time? Allow yourself the option of declining vacation requests subject to personnel requirements and production schedules.

State your policy on whether employees who leave the company voluntarily will be reimbursed for vacation time earned or whether they will forfeit vacation benefits.

- *Various other benefits*—Explain your policy, eligibility and/or availability of:

  - *Meals and snacks*—Employee lunchroom or designated eating areas, vending machines, and/or discounts on food or beverages.

  - *Employee referral program*—Will compensation be made to employees successfully recruiting worker(s) who prove to be an asset to your organization?

  - *Tuition reimbursement*—What is your policy on tuition reimbursement? What request forms or approvals are needed to qualify for tuition reimbursement?

  - *Seminars and meetings*—Most companies encourage employees to attend seminars relating to their areas of responsibility. If you encourage such activity, what must an employee do to qualify for reimbursement? What limitations or restrictions will you enforce?

  - *Statutory benefits*—This is a simple list of the benefits employees are entitled to by law which are administered by governmental agencies. Such benefits include worker's compensation, social security and unemployment compensation.

Clarifying Policy on Leaves of Absence

Under what conditions may employees take leaves of absence? What is the maximum time allowed? Can extensions be requested?

- *Disability leave (including maternity)*—If you separate the listings for disability and maternity leave, be sure the length of time you allow for each is identical. (Some attorneys advise companies to group the two together with a single list of qualifiers so there can be no allegations of inequities.) Will the employee be required to complete or sign any papers to qualify for leave? Do you want to reserve the right to require a physical examination by a company-appointed doctor during the leave of absence? Will you require the employee to sign an intent-to-return-to-work form before beginning the leave of absence?

- *Jury duty*—State that management recognizes the need for responsible United States citizens to serve on jury duty when called upon to do so. State which employee classifications will be granted time off when summoned for jury duty and any minimum length of employment required to qualify. Many companies reimburse employees who serve on a jury for the difference between jury pay and the employee's regular pay, provided time served is on a regularly scheduled workday. You may set a maximum time you will allow this arrangement without suspension of benefits.

- *Bereavement leave*—You are not obligated by law to pay employees when they miss work due to the death of a family member. It is, however, common practice to allow three days off, with pay, for regular full-time employees when there is a death in the immediate family. Some companies allow additional days off, without pay, if requested and approved. Be certain to define "immediate family" or you will find yourself paying for aunts, uncles, cousins and step-relatives. A common definition of immediate family includes husband or wife, children, parents, grandparents, brother, sister, father-in-law, mother-in-law, and grandchildren.

- *Military service*—A simple statement here will suffice. State that your company grants military leave in accordance with applicable state and federal requirements, plus any additional benefits you as an employer wish to give.

Stressing the Importance of Safety

Safety is everyone's responsibility. Urge employees to be alert to safety hazards and report them to their supervisors. Make it clear that all employees are expected to cooperate in all matters relating to safety and proper use of equipment.

General Safety Rules and Regulations at Your Company

Encouraging employees to submit safety suggestions will help raise their awareness of the need for safety; their suggestions may prevent costly accidents.

Include a list of safety rules that apply to your company or organization. For example:

- Each employee shall comply with occupational safety and health standards and all rules, regulations and orders that are applicable to his/her own action and conduct.

- All unsafe conditions should be reported to a supervisor immediately.

Personal Conduct

Restate that all employment at your company can be terminated at-will. The following list includes some types of behavior that may result in termination. This list is not all inclusive and does not affect or restrict the company's right to terminate employment at-will.

Unacceptable behavior includes but is not limited to:

- Running or traveling in an unsafe manner on company property

- Fighting on company property

- Possession or use of weapons on company time or property.

Good Housekeeping (optional)

Encourage employees to maintain a clean work environment for reasons of safety and an increased sense of pride. List a few common sense suggestions as reminders.

For example: "All work areas and aisles must be kept clear of cartons, stock and debris."

Fire Prevention

Each year thousands of businesses are damaged by fire. Urge your employees to be alert to potential hazards and report them at once. Explain how fires should be reported and list rules you expect to be followed.

For example: "In case of smoke or fire, notify the nearest member of management, giving location and other necessary information. If no member of management is present, call the local fire department. The number is prominently displayed by each telephone." (If you state that the numbers are prominently displayed, be certain correct numbers are listed by each telephone.)

Solicitation and Distribution of Literature

If you include statements forbidding solicitation and distribution of literature on company time and company property, clarify that this means "solicitations for all purposes." A statement of this type will help avoid wasted work time and prevent distribution of union-related literature on your premises. To give the statement some authority add, "Violators will be disciplined up to and including dismissal."

Procedures to Follow in the Event of a Crisis

Include information here that will contribute to the overall safety and well-being of your workers and/or help prevent employee litigation. Writing this section will help you think of precautions to prevent such occurrences as well as information you need to communicate to your employees. Once you have written the procedures, review them with supervisors, incorporate their suggestions, and then communicate the procedures to all employees. Do not rely on supervisors or employees to read and interpret procedures for themselves. Suggested topics include:

- *Employee accident*—Tell employees what to do, what not to do, who to notify, and how to document the records. Make sure all employees know where first-aid kits are located. Issue a list of emergency phone numbers to every worker; include with it the exact street address of your facility along with nearest cross streets to aid workers in relaying information to emergency dispatchers.

- *Robbery*—Urge employees not to be heroes and to never endanger themselves, a co-worker or a customer under any circumstances. Give employees full instructions on what actions are to be taken.

- *Burglary*—Tell employees what to do if it appears the store, office or plant may have been burglarized prior to their arrival at work.

- *Fire*—Be sure you have an adequate number of working fire extinguishers located throughout your facility and that workers are taught how to use them. Post your correct address by telephones so that even a new or distressed employee could give correct information under duress. At a meeting that includes all employees, thoroughly explain the procedures to be followed in the event of a fire.

Information on Personnel Issues

Tell employees that personnel files are maintained containing factual information on topics such as employee start date, wages, performance, on-the-job accidents, reports of disciplinary action, recognition and awards.

Emphasize that employees are responsible for providing current information on their home addresses, telephone numbers, marital status and other information relating to personnel, payroll deductions and dependency status. Employees may review their own file in the presence of a person designated by management, provided they schedule an appointment in advance.

Spelling Out Performance Reviews and Merit Increases

Tell employees how frequently they can expect to be reviewed and that their reviews will provide information about performance based on their job description and company policies. State that salary increases and promotions are neither guaranteed nor left to chance but directly reflect the company's view of performance and individual merit. Do not commit to more frequent reviews than you can actually fulfill.

Resolving Employee Problems

Express that work-related problems or misunderstandings occur in every organization. All such issues are important to management, and employees deserve a full opportunity to discuss conflicts and get answers.

- *Employee complaints*—Address this issue with a statement such as, "The following procedure allows employees to bring problems or complaints to the company for review and resolution: (followed by Step A, Step B, etc.)." You may want workers to begin with their immediate supervisor and proceed to a meeting with their supervisor and a department manager. If the issue is not resolved in the first two meetings, the employee would have the right to request of the department manager that a person of higher rank in the organization meet with all concerned. All conflict-resolution meetings should be properly documented.

- *Harassment*—As of this writing, there is no liability insurance to protect you, the employer, against harassment charges. This issue has become a legal hotbed for employers and a window of opportunity for employees seeking such openings.

  Harassment is a violation of employees' individual rights and is against the law. State explicitly that your company or organization considers it a violation of policy to harass any employee, either verbally or physically. State that your company policy on harassment applies to sexual harassment as well as any other form of harassment. Any employee who is being harassed is obligated to notify a member of management immediately. (Do not name only one individual as the person to be notified, in case that person is the one harassing the worker.)

Express your intent to ensure a safe and comfortable atmosphere for all employees; harassing another employee violates this philosophy and will not be tolerated.

State that the company will act quickly and decisively when advised of all harassment incidents. Victims will receive confidential help; offenders will be disciplined.

- *Disciplinary procedures*—State that rules and policies have been established to protect employees and company property. The company may discipline or discharge employees for violations of policy or other behavior considered unacceptable by the company. When the company elects progressive discipline, there will generally be a first, and sometimes a second, written warning.

- *Termination*—List the severance pay you will provide based on years of employment. Note that sometimes terminations result from a reduction in the work force. Employees will be given verbal notice or payment in lieu of notice. Allow your company the option of not paying severance pay when, for conduct reasons, it is not deserved. Include a statement such as, "In other cases of termination, severance pay will be determined on a case-by-case basis."

Additional Topics You May Want to Address:

- Parking

- General courtesy rules

- Grooming

- Use of company vehicles and equipment

- Employee suggestion system

- Confidentiality of sensitive information

- Dress code

- Awards and recognition

- Bulletin boards

- Telephones

- Lockers.

Include a Handbook Modification Statement

A final statement on the validity and timeliness of your employee policy manual is recommended. This should state that policies in your manual shall continue in effect until modified by federal or state law or by the company. Adjustments will be made for changing conditions and regulations.

Successfully Writing Your Employee Manual

From start to finish, through fact-checking, rewriting and proofreading, writing your company employee manual must be a group project. The project will be challenging and time-consuming. Include on your team a mix of authorized decision-makers, representatives from all employee levels, including middle management, and a person with strong grammar and writing skills to draft

the document. Also include senior as well as newer
employees for input, and communicate to all other
employees the various members of the committee who
will be representing them. When the second draft is
completed, have the writer and a member of management meet with a competent labor lawyer to review the
document point-by-point.

The First Draft

Organization and clarity in the first draft is an
absolute necessity. Concentrate on:

- Developing a comprehensive outline using this
  chapter as a guide

- Inputting information in a word processor for easy
  editing and moving blocks of text later as changes
  are made

- Including all the information as a basis for review
  and discussion by the group

- Communicating in simple, direct language.

Revising and Editing the Original Draft

After the group reviews the original draft, many
changes will have to be made. First, input the changes.
Then, review the overall organization of the revised
draft. Once the working draft has been reorganized,
review the document for continuity, simplicity and correct grammar. Before meeting with the group, develop a
checklist for each section to help members focus on the
important issues, such as accuracy of the information
and clarity of presentation. Your second draft is now
ready for review by the committee.

After you have input the second set of changes, the
writer and an authorized decision-maker should meet

with a labor attorney. Certain changes the attorney recommends may require a decision-maker's perspective. The writer needs to hear the discussion so he/she can accurately make the recommended changes.

Consulting a Labor Attorney

Because labor law is in a continual state of change, securing the help of a competent labor attorney is an absolute necessity when developing your employee manual. Surely, if you're ever called into court by a disgruntled employee, you'll call on a labor attorney to defend you. Make it easy on yourself—and the attorney—by having your employee manual reviewed by him/her before you print and distribute it to your employees. If you don't currently have a labor lawyer, ask your attorney for the name of someone who specializes in labor law and deals with companies of your size.

The Final Rewrite

For the final rewrite you should make another checklist. This one will get you started:

- Are all changes from the attorney included?

- Are all topics in the outline included?

- Is the text organized and easy to understand?

- Is there a Table of Contents to help readers find information easily?

- Do all titles and page numbers agree with the Table of Contents?

- Are grammar, punctuation and spelling correct?

- Has a clean copy been proofed by management and two or more proofreaders so no further changes are required?

Expect the work to go through at least three drafts as a result of editing corrections and twice as many proof-readings to catch grammar, punctuation and spelling errors. Your employee manual is a very important document, worth all the time and effort required to write and produce it. As soon as the manual is completed, schedule an annual review date for the complete document.

Federal Laws Enacted to Protect Employees' Rights

When you review your edited employee manual with your labor attorney, be certain you are covered on each of the following regulations:

1. **Equal Pay Act of 1963:** It is unlawful to pay members of one sex less than members of the opposite sex for doing the same work and holding the same job.

2. **Title VII of the Civil Rights Act of 1964:** Prohibits employment discrimination on the basis of race, color, religion, sex or national origin.

3. **Age Discrimination in Employment Act of 1967:** An employer may not discriminate against people over 40 years of age unless age is a necessary requirement for the job.

4. **Occupational Safety and Health Act of 1970:** Employers must maintain a safe environment for their employees.

5. **Vietnam Era Veterans' Readjustment Assistance Act of 1972:** Employers with federal contracts of $10,000 or more must take affirmative action to hire disabled and qualified veterans of the Vietnam War.

6. **Vocational Rehabilitation Act of 1973:** Employers who have federal contracts of $2,500 or more must take affirmative action to employ and advance qualified handicapped persons.

7. **Employee Retirement Income Security Act of 1974:** Employers providing pensions for employees must establish and maintain their retirement plans according to federal minimum standards.

8. **Pregnancy Discrimination Act of 1978:** Pregnant women are protected from discrimination under the terms of Title VII of the Civil Rights Act.

9. **Immigration Reform and Control Act of 1986:** An employer may not discriminate against a job applicant on the basis of national origin or citizen status but may give preference to a U.S. citizen over an alien if both are equally qualified.

10. **Employee Polygraph Protection Act of 1988:** Most private employers cannot require or ask employees or prospective employees to take a polygraph test. Also, employers may not discipline anyone who refuses such a test.

11. **Worker Adjustment and Retraining Act of 1988:** Employers whose work force totals more than 100 employees must give their employees 60 days notification of plant closings and mass layoffs.

12. **Fair Labor Standards Act (plus several dozen federal statutes):** Employers may not discriminate or discharge employees for exercising statutory rights.

13. **Consolidated Omnibus Budget Reconciliation Act of 1985 (COBRA):** Requires health care continuation option for terminating inactive employees and

dependents, only if covered by insurance and only if the company employs more than 20 people.

14. **Americans with Disabilities Act:** Prohibits handicap discrimination in employment and requires reasonable accommodation of handicaps. Act became effective July 1992.

15. **Older Workers Benefit Protection Act:** Restricts waivers of age discrimination gains and limits age-based reduction of benefits; applies to all employees covered by Age Discrimination in Employment Act.

16. **Family Leave Act of 1993:** Requires employers to provide unpaid leave of up to 12 weeks for each eligible employee in the event of a newborn/adopted child, acute medical needs of an immediate family member, or an employee's own illness.

CHAPTER 9

NOW YOU CAN WRITE MORE DYNAMIC REPORTS AND MEMOS

Why It Pays to Improve Your Writing Skills

Like it or not, we're all judged in part by our ability to communicate on paper. Look around at our nation's greatest leaders. It's no coincidence that their words have style, clarity and impact. Even if you're not running for president, you'll still benefit from improving your writing skills. As you practice the techniques presented in this report, you'll find that the same skills used to write more dynamic reports will apply to other kinds of writing, too.

As you develop reports using the methods presented here, you'll find:

*   Your thinking and your ability to articulate your thoughts will improve. You'll learn to spot relevant material and report it logically and sequentially.

*   You'll develop and use a more powerful vocabulary.

*   You'll weed out the clutter from your first drafts, leaving strong, clear statements.

*   Your peers and supervisors will recognize your improved communication skills. As your reports become more dynamic and powerful, you too will be more highly regarded.

How Reports Differ from Other
Forms of Writing

Reports differ from memos and everyday letters in several ways:

- Reports often include quantifiable data, which can be presented in tables or charts or depicted in graphs.

- Reports often require information beyond the facts at hand.

- Reports are usually—but not always—longer than letters or memos.

- Reports are written in more formal language than that of most letters or memos.

- Reports, like letters, may be written to just one person, but often they are read by several people.

How the Writing Process Differs for Reports

Since reports are longer, more serious and more fact-oriented than other forms of written communication, they are also more difficult to write.

In a well-written report, the style looks smooth and natural—but don't be fooled. Writing this way actually takes a great deal of effort, a few specific skills, and at least one or two rough drafts. However, you can develop good writing skills over time using the same techniques employed by professional business communicators. And, you'll begin to reap the benefits of your newly developed skills almost immediately.

How to Write Dynamic Reports

Below are step-by-step directions for writing more dynamic reports. You do not have to complete all steps in one sitting, but you will benefit from following all the steps.

Step 1: Write down the objective(s) of your report.

List no more than three. Your objectives should be measurable and realistic. Putting your objectives on paper will force you to think through the purpose of your report. Are you writing to inform? to force a decision? to persuade your audience to your point of view? Below are two examples of suitable objectives:

Example 1:

To persuade the top five executives of XYZ Co. to approve the purchase of a new micro-computer for the personnel department.

Example 2:

To convince the company president of the need to amend the 1990-91 advertising budget.

Step 2: Identify your audience.

What binds them together? What are their values and beliefs? Even if you're writing to inform or persuade, write from your audience's point of view.

As you begin writing your report, formulating written objectives and learning about your audience will help you:

• Select only relevant information

• Arrange facts and data to support your objectives

- Write more clearly and concisely.

Step 3: Draft a temporary outline.

Ask yourself what you already know about your topic and what information will require outside resources. List your own questions and those that your audience might want answered.

Then arrange what you already know with what you need to know into an outline. As you learn more about your topic through additional research, your outline will evolve to reflect your increased knowledge.

Step 4: Research your topic thoroughly, using up-to-date resources.

The people who read your report will be counting on you for accurate research and reliable information. Research can be laborious and time-consuming, but it is too important to be short-changed.

To streamline the research process, list the information you need to gather. Then determine where you might find this information. The goal is to minimize your research time by seeking information from the best sources.

Gather more information than you will actually include in your report. Your words will carry greater authority when you are armed with current, reliable information; and, the more material you have to choose from, the more selective you can be.

Sources of information include the following:

- Friends, associates, co-workers
- Company records
- Public and university libraries

*   On-line databases

*   Public relations departments

*   Annual reports

*   Associations

*   Government printing offices

*   Seminars and workshops.

Note all sources used. If your information is from a conversation, note the name of the person with whom you spoke plus any other substantiating information, such as title or affiliation. If your information is from a written source, document the title, page number, author, publisher and publication date.

To use a direct quote from another person, such as in a speech, you must first get written permission. When you use material from a printed source, like a magazine article, you must use it precisely as it was written and credit the source in your report.

Plagiarism, or "lifting" material without crediting the source, is unethical. You may paraphrase; that is, express the same general idea in your own words, or draw your own conclusions as the result of consulting several sources. Both of these practices are regarded as highly acceptable by the academic and business worlds.

Step 5: Write the first draft using your outline as a guide.

Here are a few pointers to keep in mind as you complete the first draft:

*   Define key terms your audience may not understand.

Suppose you were writing to a group of accountants. It would not be necessary to define terms like current cost, current value accounting and depreciable cost.

But if you were using these same terms in a report for engineers and their understanding hinged on knowing what these words meant, you would want to include a glossary of key terms. If you need to define only two or three words, it is simpler to define them within the text of your report.

Your report will make more of an impact on the reader if the message is easy to grasp. To accomplish this task, provide your readers with complete and accurate information.

- Present your ideas in the order that most effectively conveys your message.

  Here are several options:

  - Start with the most important point(s) and progress to the least important. This inverted pyramid style is common in newspaper journalism because it allows the writer to communicate information quickly and clearly.

  - Present ideas or describe events in chronological order. Use this method whenever it's important for your reader to know the sequence of events, such as the history of a company or the reporting of an accident.

  - Present concepts by item or group according to location or in a linear progression. For example, if you were discussing the happenings at various plants across the country, you might discuss them in order from east coast to west coast rather than skipping all around.

- Work from large to small or vice versa. Use this technique when discussing, for example, accounts of varying sizes or sales goals.

- Work from the easy or known to the more difficult or unknown. When introducing new material, build on what your audience already knows—then show how the new material relates.

- Present a procedure in the order it is performed. This method is similar to the chronological method, but it refers to giving someone instructions for completing a task, such as reconciling a bank account or assembling a piece of equipment. Provide numbered, step-by-step instructions.

Step 6: Revise and edit.

In your first draft, you concentrated on "the big picture." Now that you have your ideas down on paper, go back and strengthen your writing. Here are a few tips:

- Replace passive verbs with active verbs.

   Note the difference in these two examples:

   Example 1:

   Work stations will be kept neater when mail is handled and sorted promptly. (passive)

   Example 2:

   Open and sort mail promptly to help maintain neat work stations. (active)

   Sentences using active verbs convey the same information with fewer words and greater strength.

- Make every word count.

Good business writing should be simple, clear and concise. Write to express rather than impress. For example:

Instead of saying:	Say:
In the event of	If
Owing to the fact that	Because
For a period of a month	For a month

Weed out weak words and replace them with words that evoke accurate mental images. For example, instead of saying, "Profits went up a lot," say, "Profits soared." As a rule of thumb, replace verbs and adverbs (words often ending in "-ly") with action verbs. Here are some more examples:

Weak verb phrases	Action verbs
left abruptly	fled
dropped quickly	plummeted
asked suspiciously	interrogated

• Keep the tone of your report compatible with your topic.

Set the tone at the beginning of your report, then avoid doing anything to contradict that tone. Otherwise, your reader may become confused. Likewise, avoid introducing extraneous thoughts since these, too, might distract your audience or confuse them. Include only that information which serves a purpose within the report.

• Make sure your writing does the job.

Ask yourself these questions:

    • Does the draft follow the outline?

- If not, does the outline need to be changed or does the draft?

- Does the presentation of the material follow the logical sequence I've decided to use?

- Have I included any unnecessary information?

- Is the punctuation correct? spelling? grammar?

- Is each sentence tight—crisp—concise?

Step 7: Decide whether to include tables, charts, graphs, diagrams or other illustrations.

Ask yourself :

- Will one or more visuals enhance the message or the appearance of my report?

- Which points could most benefit from the support of a visual?

- What kind of visual will best depict what I have to say? A pie chart? A bar or line graph? A more creative graphic?

- Am I capable of producing the visual(s) myself, or will I need help?

Step 8: Determine the format of your report.

If the report is longer than one page, insert one or more headings to make it more visually appealing and reader-friendly. If you use more than one type of heading, be sure that similar headings (e.g., all capitals, or underlined upper and lowercase headings) convey similar levels of information. See the following example.

OUTLINE
Proofreading Report

I. The Importance of Accurate Proofreading
   A. Company Image
   B. Proofreader's Job
   C. Reader's Understanding
II. The Steps of Accurate Proofreading
   A. Grammar
      1. Subject
      2. Pronoun
      3. Verb
   B. Spelling

The report headings from this outline might look like this:

IMPROVING YOUR PROOFREADING SKILLS

The Importance of Accurate Proofreading

   Company Image

   Proofreader's Job

   Reader's Understanding

The Steps of Accurate Proofreading

   Grammar

      Subject

      Pronoun

      Verb

   Spelling

Printed material is more inviting to read when there is an ample amount of white space on the page. A full page of single-spaced type will discourage even those who like to read.

If you're using a simple typewriter, you can still make your report visually appealing through centering, underlining, and incorporating caps and bold type into your report. If you have access to a word processor, your options increase. And if you're blessed with a desktop publishing system, your options are almost endless! Be careful, however—don't get so clever that the format of your report detracts from your message. Keep the format simple, and limit typestyles within a document.

Step 9: Edit one more time with your most critical eye.

Ask yourself the following questions:

- Have I met my goals and objectives?

- Have I answered all questions and addressed all issues listed in my outline?

- Is my material arranged in the most logical sequence?

- Does the information flow smoothly from one paragraph to the next?

- Is all the necessary information included under the proper heading?

- Have I made it easy for my readers to grasp the main points of my report?

- Is the tone of my report appropriate and consistent throughout?

- Do the visuals enhance and support the written material?

- Are the graphs, charts, illustrations and tables accurate? Are they properly labeled for maximum clarity?

• Do the visuals convey the information intended?

• Does my report look inviting to read?

When you've answered "yes" to all of these questions, you're ready for the final step.

Step 10: Proofread!

The importance of proofreading cannot be stressed enough. Check for accuracy and also to make sure no information has been accidentally omitted. Now is the time to spot errors, not after you've already printed final copies of your report. Ask two other people in your office to proofread your document—one for content and accuracy, and one for grammar, spelling and punctuation. After working on a particular document for a long time, you'll be less likely to spot errors.

Correct any errors, print the document, package in appropriate binders or covers and deliver copies to your readers.

How to Write Effective Memos

Memorandums, or memos, are the most common type of interoffice communications. Memos have many advantages over verbal communication. For example, memos can be sent to several persons simultaneously. They also provide a written record for the sender and recipient.

Memos are commonly used to:

• Make announcements

• Request information

• Give instructions

- Introduce another piece of communication, such as a report.

Writing the Introduction

To make your memo clear from the start, use this standard format:

TO:

FROM:

DATE:

SUBJECT: (or RE:)

State the subject of your memo (what the memo is regarding) in one or two lines. An example of a good introduction follows.

TO:	Mary Jane Dolens, Purchasing
FROM:	Susan Wiler, Word Processing
DATE:	August 11, 1993
SUBJECT:	Ordering larger quantities of office supplies

Providing this information up front tells the reader immediately who is sending the memo and why. It is not necessary to put a signature at the end of your memos. You might, however, want to write your initials next to your name in the introduction. And if you're sending the memo to more than one person, list their name(s) at the bottom of the memo after the caption "cc:," which stands for carbon copy or "pc:," which stands for photo copy.

Writing the Body of the Memo

An effective memo contains three key elements:

- The main point; that is, why the memo is being written

- Supporting evidence (sometimes this is unnecessary)

- A call to action (What do you want your reader to do as a result of your memo? Communicate this action to the reader and, when appropriate, give a deadline.)

Determine your main point(s) and remain focused throughout. Then organize your information in a way that will help the reader understand and remember your message.

"This is a pretty scathing memo, Jane. Would you mind elaborating a bit on the "pervasive herd mentality" you claim our firm is riddled with?"

When writing your memo, get right to the point. Include only the essential information, but don't leave your reader with unanswered questions.

The following is an example of a poorly written memo. Notice how it contains irrelevant information and lacks a call to action.

TO: Mary S.

FROM: Bob

DATE: August 11

SUBJECT: Bulletin board

    I want to explain something that I've noticed happening within the last two weeks. I've found that the bulletin board contains too much outdated information and unauthorized information. As you know, the board must be checked weekly and all outdated information must be discarded. I saw something on there yesterday that was a month old! Also, I must approve of all information before it is placed on the board. No one is allowed to place "personal ads" such as the one I saw last week that said "Tent for Sale." The bulletin board is for company matters only. I'm giving a copy of this memo to Sarah so she knows how to handle the board when you're on vacation.

On the following page is that same memo rewritten for greater clarity. Notice how much easier it is to read, and how it contains a specific call to action.

TO: Mary Salenger

FROM: Bob Green

DATE: August 11, 1993

SUBJECT: Posting and removing outdated/unauthorized information from the bulletin board

Within the last two weeks I've noticed the bulletin board contains outdated and unauthorized information. To eliminate this problem:

1. Check the bulletin board every Friday and discard any information that's more than a week old or no longer relevant.

2. Get my verbal approval before placing any documents on the board.

I'm sending Sarah Jones a copy of this memo so she'll know how to handle the bulletin board when you're on vacation.

Thank you.

cc: Sarah Jones

If your memo is longer than one page, divide it into sections with a brief heading for each one. Dividing your memo into sections enables your readers to scan the memo before reading, organize your information, and reread selected portions without searching the entire document.

Listing Items

Use bullet points to display a series of items neatly and efficiently. For example:

The following tasks have been completed:

- Typing the Johnson report
- Filing last week's proposals
- Ordering computer supplies
- Placing a classified ad for a salesperson.

Giving Instructions

When giving instructions, use numbered steps so the reader knows the correct sequence for completing the task and will be less likely to skip a step. For example:

Before telling a caller I'm not in:

1. Check the sign-out sheet to see if I've signed out, and note the time I'm expected back, in case the caller asks.

2. If I have not signed out, check to see if I'm in my office.

3. If you cannot reach me in my office, page me.

4. If I have not signed out, and I cannot be reached using steps 2 or 3, take a message and tell the caller I will return the call as soon as possible.

All your memos will convey your messages effectively if you remember to:

- Start your memo with the standard memo introduction. Be sure to state your subject clearly and concisely.

- Get to the point of your memo quickly.

- Include only essential information—but don't leave the reader guessing.

- Organize your information in a logical sequence.

- Divide lengthy memos into sections with brief headings that highlight your main points for the reader.

- Include a call to action, and a deadline when appropriate.

Improving Your Writing Skills

The theory that some people are born writers and others are not has yet to be proven. People who say they can't write usually mean they're uncomfortable writing; they simply haven't developed good writing skills.

The good news is these skills can be learned. Anybody can write dynamic reports and memos. All it takes is discipline and practice. Start by implementing the advice presented here and soon you'll be reaping the rewards of improved writing skills: better, more effective communication and the respect of your colleagues and co-workers.

CHAPTER 10

PRECISION WRITING MADE EASY

Nearly all writing can be improved with added precision. You need it whenever you convey written facts to someone else. A memo distributed within an organization is a common example of writing requiring precision. Memos are not meant to entertain; rather, they are meant to inform employees of happenings within the organization. To properly convey your meaning memos must contain accurate information and relay it in a clear and concise manner. This is the basis of precision writing: to communicate factual information accurately, clearly and objectively to your intended audience.

More obvious forms of precision writing include research data written by medical professionals, police reports detailing crimes, structural details written by engineers and architects, and proposals, bids, specifications or instructional manuals used by tradespeople. Because precision writing describes processes, it must be accurate and clear so readers can carry out your instructions.

Hazards arise from writing that is inaccurate, ambiguous or difficult for the reader to understand. If facts are inaccurate, research data may be used incorrectly by doctors; building specifications may create havoc for contractors; software instructions may cause users to delete the wrong file. Even if the information is accurate yet presented in an unclear manner, the same hazards can occur; the reader may misunderstand and, therefore, misuse your information. Worse yet, the reader may not understand your information enough to even begin using it.

On the other hand, the benefits of accurate and clear writing are enormous:

- In-house policies and procedures are understood and followed by all employees, increasing productivity and reducing errors.

- Your proposals are easily understood and more likely to be accepted.

- Your brochures catch customers' attention and list easy-to-understand benefits.

- Clear and professional writing enhances your company's image.

- Smooth communication ensures all parties derive the same message.

- Your customers can easily follow your product instructions; this results in fewer calls for assistance, saving you time and money.

Your Readers

Precision writing is easier when you know who your readers are. Discern what they already understand about your subject, then match your writing to their level. Before you begin writing, answer the following questions:

- What is the objective of my document? To teach? To inform? To persuade?

- Who will be reading my document?

- What is their background in this subject?

- How much do they already know about my subject?

- Is the information they've learned about my subject correct?

- How will readers use this information?

- What specific information do they need to know?

- What format would be most helpful to them? (e.g. short report, long detailed report, illustrations or descriptions.)

Once you answer these questions, you can plan a document tailored to your readers' exact needs. Try to build on what they already know. If you cannot identify all your readers, tailor your writing to those who are least knowledgeable in your subject. This way everyone in your audience will understand your document and those familiar with the material can skim parts of it.

Feedback

Before printing your final draft, let someone read your document and give you feedback on organization and clarity. Ask them to test any instructions you wrote to see if they are accurate and easy to follow. Make necessary changes based on their feedback. You may also want to consult the "Precision Writing Checklist" at the end of this chapter before beginning your document.

What Are the Elements of Precision Writing?

Outlines

List your ideas in the most logical sequence and create an outline of your document before you begin writing. Examine it to ensure your ideas are arranged in an easy-to-follow order. If they are not, now is the time to rearrange them on your outline instead of rearranging your paragraphs or pages later.

The more detailed your outline is, the better. Follow it as you write your document so you can anticipate what is covered in the next paragraph and lead into it.

Outlines make writing much easier because you've already planned the material you will cover and the sequence in which it will be covered. All that's left is filling in the information. The following is an example of an outline:

PAPER RECYCLING

I.   Types of Paper Accepted
  A.   Newspaper
  B.   Magazines
  C.   Cardboard
  D.   Office Paper
     1.   Copy machine paper
     2.   Computer paper

II. Drop-Off Sites
  A.   32nd Street & Airport Road
  B.   2345 Baltimore Avenue
  C.   4578 Eastern Avenue

III. Recycling Companies
  A.   Johnston & Tinzler
  B.   Barker, Inc.
  C.   Second Time Paper
     1.   Second Time - 1222 Franklin Street
     2.   Second Time - 5664 Hampton Blvd.

Paragraphs

Make your document readable by keeping paragraphs short—no more than 14 lines in length. Long paragraphs will tire your reader and your main idea may become lost.

Begin each paragraph with an introduction that states the purpose or central idea of your paragraph. Explain your central idea using detailed information and examples in the paragraph body. Summarize the main point in the paragraph's conclusion for final clarification. You may also lead into the next paragraph by ending with a statement that serves as a transition.

Example of a well-structured paragraph:

> Effective managers need to be leaders willing to help employees develop their potential. As leaders, effective managers set an example and attract willing followers who strive to work up to the leader's expectations. They also praise workers for their contributions and offer constructive criticism when appropriate. Managers with leadership abilities cultivate productive and satisfied employees who could potentially become leaders themselves some day. Yet how many companies fail to invest in their future leaders?

Sentences

Present only one idea per sentence to make your writing clear and understandable. This lets your reader absorb the information before moving on to the next idea. If your sentence extends more than three lines, try to make it more concise or divide it into more than one sentence. Follow the eight tips presented below for more concise sentences

Tip #1: Use the fewest number of words necessary to make your point.

Instead of writing: "At this point in time we are unable to determine the probable cause of the damage."

Write: "We do not yet know what caused the damage."

Notice how the second sentence eliminates unnecessary words and phrases but retains the same meaning.

Tip #2: Use an informal, conversational writing style.

A formal style may cloud your meaning and seem impersonal.

Formal: "It seems difficult to inform someone of their inadequate performance."

Informal: "It is hard to tell someone they performed badly."

Tip #3: Whenever possible, use the active voice.

The active voice will make your writing stronger and more direct than the passive voice.

Passive: "The meeting will be arranged by us this week."

Active: "We will arrange the meeting this week."

Do you see how the active sentence is more clear and concise than the passive one?

Tip #4: Use the active voice when giving instructions.

Passive: "After eating lunch, the table should be cleaned."

Active: "Clean the table after lunch."

The passive sentence is not directed at the reader, making it unclear as to who must clean the table. The active sentence is direct and clearly tells the reader what action he or she must take.

Tip #5: Avoid beginning sentences with the word "there" or "it."

These words often clutter the sentence instead of adding meaning to it.

Instead of writing: "There are many personnel issues that need to be discussed in the meeting."

Write: "Many personnel issues need to be discussed in the meeting."

Instead of writing: "It was the Nobel Prize that she was awarded."

Write: "She was awarded the Nobel Prize."

Tip #6: Avoid using the phrase "to be," which also adds clutter.

Remove "to be" from the following sentences:

He seems (to be) intelligent.

The storm appeared (to be) severe.

Tip #7: Use the present tense in most writing.

Avoid using future tense and conditional tense with "should," "would" or "could."

Instead of writing: "The security system would fail if it had insufficient power."

Write: "The security system fails with insufficient power."

Tip #8: Turn negatives into positives.

Negative: "We did not find anything wrong with the car."

Positive: "We found nothing wrong with the car."

Negative: "I don't have any glasses."

Positive: "I have no glasses."

The second sentence in each group gets right to the point using fewer words.

Words and Phrases

Shorten phrases into single words when possible:

in order to	➔	to
at this point in time	➔	now
due to the fact that	➔	because
has the ability to	➔	can
the majority of	➔	most
take the place of	➔	substitute
prior to that time	➔	before

The following words and phrases are unnecessary and can be completely eliminated:

- first and foremost
- as a matter of fact
- hither to
- perchance
- whereby
- aforementioned
- needless to say
- inasmuch
- thereof
- whereas
- thereby

Use simple words rather than complex ones:

utilize	➔	use
obtain	➔	get
subsequent	➔	next
terminate	➔	end
conjecture	➔	guess
commence	➔	begin
demonstrate	➔	show

Avoid using "jargon," or words understood only by those in your field.

Economists would understand: "Figures will be out today on the CPI."

Others need to hear: "Figures will be out today on the Consumer Price Index."

If you must use jargon, provide definitions for those readers who may not understand.

Avoid redundancy by eliminating words that have the same meaning as other words in the sentence.

Redundant: "The report's final conclusion was positive."

Better: "The report's conclusion was positive."

Other redundant examples include:

first priority	➜	priority
honest truth	➜	truth
small in size	➜	small
true facts	➜	facts
different varieties	➜	varieties
take action	➜	act
continue on	➜	continue
basic essentials	➜	essentials
good asset	➜	asset

What Is the Best Page Format?

The format of your document is just as important as the information it contains. You motivate people to read your material when you use a correct and consistent format throughout.

General Organization

Make your document as easy to read as possible. Help readers find specific sections by providing a table of contents, headings and subheadings, page numbers and section numbers. Lengthy reports may even require glossaries and appendices to give readers extra help with definitions and examples that support your information.

Headings and Subheadings

Break up your material by inserting headings and subheadings. These smaller sections make your document appear more readable and less intimidating. Also, headings allow readers to scan your material for an overview before they begin reading.

Readers rely on headings to guide them through your material and help them find specific sections. Therefore, keep headings brief but informative, and be consistent with their placement.

Make headings and subheadings stand out by putting them in bold print, in all capital letters or by underlining them. Be consistent with your use of styles. Inconsistency detracts from your information and makes your document appear unorganized. Use a style sheet to easily remember heading styles. A style sheet is a guide sheet on which you display the heading style for each level of information. Some computer programs allow you to use a style sheet while formatting documents, which saves many steps.

Use no more than four levels of headings. More levels will confuse the reader and defeat your purpose. If you are unable to use different fonts to set your headings and subheadings apart, use all caps, underlining or bold type instead.

All headings must be consistent, or parallel, for each level. If your level two begins with a verb ending in "-ing." all level two headings throughout the document must be worded the same, like "Removing a Paper Jam." Similar headings contribute to the conciseness and clarity of your document.

Numbered Steps

Use numbered steps to describe a step-by-step procedure. This makes each task clear and simple and helps the reader complete the tasks in the correct order. Also, numbering makes it easy to refer to "step 3" if clarification is necessary.

For example:

1. Press the "On" button.
2. Turn the dial to "1."
3. Insert the paper into the self-feed slot to the right.
4. Repeat step 3 for the number of sheets required

Keep steps parallel with one another as the above list illustrates. Parallel steps consistently use the same parts of speech. The above steps are parallel because they each begin with a command, directing the reader to action. Statements that begin with verbs like "press," "turn," or "lift" are the most effective when giving instructions. These statements clearly tell readers what action they must take to accomplish a task.

Bulleted Lists

When sequence is not important, place information in a bulleted list. This makes the information easy to read and understand.

For example:

Features of our copy machine include:

- Low noise level

- Easy-to-reach toner cartridge

- Large paper capacity

- Two paper trays

Notice these points are also parallel; each is a phrase beginning with an adjective.

White Space

White space is the amount of blank space on a page. Pages with adequate white space are more inviting to your reader because the pages are easy to read. The example on the right is an effective use of white space.

HEADING

xxxxxxxxxxxxxxxxxxxxx
xxxxxxxxxxxxxxxxxxxxx
xxxxxxxxxxxxxxxxxxxxx
xxxxxxxxxxxxxxxxxxxxx
xxxxxxxxxxxxxxxxxxxxx
Subheading

xxxxxxxxxxxxxxxxxxxxx
xxxxxxxxxxxxxxxxxxxxx
xxxxxxxxxxxxxxxxxxxxx
xxxxxxxxxxxxxxxxxxxxx
xxxxxxxxxxxxxxxxx
xxxxxxxxxxxxxxxxxxxxx
xxxxxxxxxxxxxxxxxxxxx
xxxxxxxxxxxxxxxxxxxxx

This example is easy to read because the white space is on the left side of the page and the heading is aligned with the text. The subheading on the left allows for easy scanning.

This example is diffi-
cult to read because the
headings are centered.
Reading is slowed when
the eyes must jump back
and forth from centered
headings to flush-left text
(text that begins at the left
margin.)

HEADING

xxxxxxxxxxxxxxxxxxxx
xxxxxxxxxxxxxxxxxxxx
xxxxxxxxxxxxxxx

SUBHEADING

xxxxxxxxxxxxxxxxxxxx
xxxxxxxxxxxxxxxxxxxx
xxxxxxxxxxxx
xxxxxxxxxxxxxxxxxxxx
xxxxxxxxxxxxxxxxxxxx
xxxxxxxxxxxxxxxxxxxx
xxxxxxx

SUBHEADING

xxxxxxxxxxxxxxxxxxxx
xxxxxxxxxxxxxxxxxxxx

Value of Visuals

If you have the capability of preparing flow charts,
they are often the clearest way to present step-by-step
instructions. Consider the following example:

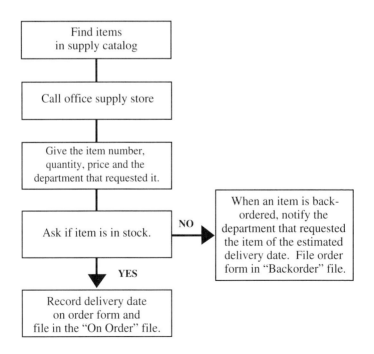

What Are Typical Uses for Precision Writing?

Precision writing is typically used in business settings or wherever coherence is of the utmost importance. Writing computer software manuals, policy and procedure manuals, manufacturing procedures and office procedures requires precision.

Computer Software Manuals

Know the Software Users

Whenever possible, it helps to know who your users are so your manual helps them and enhances the software. Find out who your users are and what types of jobs they hold. If possible, ask them their purpose for using the software; then you will be able to write a manual that helps them achieve their purpose. Begin by:

- *Establishing a profile of your audience*—Who they are, what types of jobs they hold, and what their objectives are when using your manual.

- *Establishing your objective*—To give an overview? To instruct? To help readers achieve proficiency?

- *Establishing sequence through use of an outline*—Be sure to cover all necessary points to meet your objectives and the needs of your audience.

Keep It Clear and Simple

Keep your writing clear and simple. Strive for the cookbook approach when describing sequential tasks.

---

1. Add 1 tsp. margarine and 1 tsp. of salt.

2. Cover the pan.

3. Simmer for 10 to 15 minutes on low heat.

Begin sentences with verbs as in the following example. Each statement clearly names the action the reader must take. Each task is separated into a manageable function so the user has to deal with only a small amount of information at a time.

Effective instructions for a software process:

---

1. Press [C] to clear your screen.

2. Type the word "EXIT."

3. Press [RETURN].

4. Remove your diskette from Drive A.

The numbered steps are direct and easy to follow. Notice how keys are placed in brackets and quotation marks indicate words the user needs to type. Once you establish a style for items like keys and words the user must type, maintain consistency throughout your document.

Answer the following questions in order when writing procedures for a software manual:

1. What is the process?

2. How does the process work?

3. What is an example of this process?

4. What are the step-by-step instructions for this process?

See how the following example from a computer software manual addresses these questions:

MOVING TEXT

The "Move" function removes a section of your text from its original location and places it in a new location. Simply highlight the section you want to move then press [MOVE]. Next, place the cursor where you want the text to appear and press [ENTER].

For example, in the following paragraph, the first sentence needs to be moved to the end of the paragraph:

Although the diameter of the pipe is wide enough to fit the fixture, it is not made from the proper material. It is unsafe to use this pipe with the fixture.

After executing the [MOVE] function, the paragraph reads:

It is unsafe to use this pipe with the fixture. Although the diameter of the pipe is wide enough to fit the fixture, it is not made from the proper material.

The [MOVE] function is a fast and easy way to move text without deleting it and retyping it in another location.

Follow these step-by-step instructions to move a section of your text:

1. Place the cursor at the beginning of the section you want to move.

2. Press the arrow keys to highlight the section.

3. Press [MOVE].

4. Place the cursor where you want that section to begin again.

5. Press [ENTER] to position text in its new location.

Policy and Procedure Manuals

The rules of precision writing are important in policy and procedure manuals. Everyone must derive the same meaning from your policies and procedures in order to understand and follow them in the manner you intended. Your manuals will be more clearly understood if you keep in mind that a policy is a rule; it describes what the rule is. A procedure tells how one accomplishes a task.

Before writing a policy and procedure manual, know your audience and write to their level of understanding. Also ask yourself what the company wants the manual to accomplish. This helps you know what information to include and the best way to express it.

Be as thorough and complete as possible. Cover all aspects of the policy or procedure, leaving no questions in the reader's mind. Have several people critique your manual to see if the meanings are clear.

This policy is unclear:

If you have a baby, you will receive six weeks off.

It leaves many questions in the reader's mind and is open to different interpretations:

- When does one receive six weeks off? Before, during or after the pregnancy?

- Is this paid or unpaid time off?

- Will the same job be retained?

- Does this policy apply to mothers and fathers?

Also, the statement implies that six and only six weeks of time will be given; it is unclear whether the employee must take this amount of time off from work or has the option of taking less time.

A much clearer policy reads:

Mothers and fathers are allowed up to six weeks of unpaid maternity leave, beginning before or immediately following their baby's birth. They will resume their same position upon return to work.

Here is an example of an unclear procedure:

To request time off, fill out a request form, have it signed and give it to the personnel office.

This procedure also leaves many questions in the reader's mind:

- Time off for what? Vacation, dentist appointment or any time off?

- Where are the request forms?

- Who signs the request form and why?

- Where, and to whom, in the personnel office do you take the form?

A much clearer procedure is:

To request time off for appointments, vacations or leaves of absence:

1. Pick up a Time-off Request form in the mail room. Fill out the form; include all requested information.

2. Turn in your request to your immediate supervisor at least three days before your requested time off is to begin.

3. Your request will be approved or denied, depending on work schedules and available vacation time. You will be notified of the decision.

4. If your request is denied and you feel it is an unreasonable denial, see Section 5 of this manual, "How to Register a Complaint."

Manufacturing Procedures

Manufacturing procedures instruct employees on the exact steps for completing a manufacturing process. It is essential to write clear and precise procedures so employees can follow the steps correctly, completely and safely, and produce a high-quality product as a result.

Separate steps into simple, manageable parts. Make sure they are in the correct sequence.

Example from a manufacturing procedures manual:

To attach a reducer bushing to a tub spout:

1. Cover your hands with protective gloves.

2. Place the reducer bushing on the bushing fixture.

3. Place the tub spout over the bushing fixture.

4. Press down firmly on the spout until the buzzer sounds.

5. Lift the tub spout from the bushing fixture and quickly check if the reducer bushing is in place.

If the reducer bushing is in place:

1. Set the tub spout on the conveyor belt then begin again with step one for the next spout.

If the reducer bushing is not in place:

1. Repeat the first five steps.

2. Notify your foreman if it is still not in place.

Steps listed in a manufacturing procedures manual may require a diagram that illustrates all of the parts involved (bushing fixture, reducer bushing, tub spout). Add labels to names of parts for easy identification.

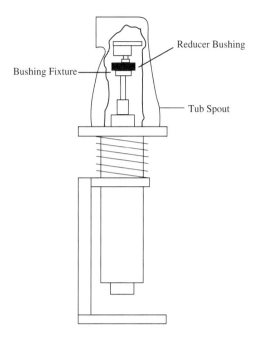

Office Procedures

Well-written office procedures are also important for efficient office operations. As with all procedures, be thorough; include each step in the proper sequence and leave no questions in the readers' minds.

Unclear office procedure:

> Properly close the office when you are the last person to leave.

Clear office procedure:

> The last person to leave the office each day must:
> 1. Lock the supply closet.
> 2. Remove key from postage meter.
> 3. Turn off the lights.
> 4. Lock the outside door.

Conveying Your Message

Whether writing is a large portion of your job or a very small portion, it's important that you write so that your readers clearly understand your intended message. This applies to interoffice communications, business proposals, manufacturing procedures, product instructions—practically every business application.

To learn more about writing for business purposes, pick up a copy of Mark Forbes's *Writing Technical Articles, Speeches, and Manuals* (USA: John Wiley & Sons, 1988). Or refer to *Technical Writing—Structure, Standards, and Style* by Gary Blake and Robert W. Bly (New York: McGraw-Hill, 1982).

It pays to polish your writing skills so that all of your messages are delivered with precision, leaving no room for doubt or misunderstanding. Say it clearly the first time, and you'll need to say it only once.

Precision Writing Checklist

After writing your outline, ask yourself these questions:

1. Is my outline arranged in a logical, easy-to-follow sequence?

2. Have I included all the reader will need to know?

3. Do I know my audience's level of understanding?

After writing your first draft ask:

1. Are my facts correct?

2. Is my writing clear and geared to my readers' level of understanding?

3. Are my sentences short, containing only one main idea?

4. Do my paragraphs have a central theme and flow smoothly, one to the other?

5. Do I use the present tense whenever possible?

6. Do I use the active voice instead of passive?

7. Do I use positives instead of negatives?

8. Do I use simple rather than complex words?

9. Is my writing clear and concise?

10. Are sequential tasks logically arranged in numbered steps?

After your first rewrite ask:

1. Are my headings, terms and symbols consistent? Is my writing style appropriate and consistent?

2. Is my document in a logical format?

3. Is the format visually appealing?

4. Have I included organizational supplements, such as a table of contents, glossary, appendix or index?

5. Do I use headings and subheadings in the appropriate places to break up my text?

6. Do I use four or fewer consistent levels of headings and subheadings to assist the reader?

7. Have I solicited feedback on my rewrite?

8. Have I had someone test my instructions for accuracy?

After checking these points, you're ready to begin your final draft. Once the final draft is printed, go over these points one more time to catch last-minute errors. Have the document proofread. Then congratulate yourself for producing a clear and concise document that your readers will understand and appreciate.

CHAPTER 11

HOW TO CONDUCT A CUSTOMER SURVEY AND ADDRESS QUALITY ISSUES HEAD-ON

The '90s promise to be a decade of positive customer and employee relations. In an effort to accomplish these objectives, people are recognizing the vital role surveys play. Properly utilized, a survey can effectively reveal how to better achieve customer satisfaction or uncover employee grievances and point the way to a more positive work environment. This chapter will help you decide whether you need to conduct a survey. Then, if you decide to do so, the information contained here will help you determine whether to conduct the survey yourself or call on a professional to help you achieve the best results from an employee attitude or customer satisfaction survey. A Glossary is included at the end of this chapter for your reference.

The Benefits

A survey, when properly conducted, is the most effective means of gathering group data, insights and opinions. You can make a survey work to your advantage by sending a letter to your target audience in advance of the survey and including a simple introductory paragraph in the questionnaire itself explaining your objective for conducting the survey. Weave it into your letter or survey introduction. Keep it conversational. For example, "One of the reasons we are conducting this survey is to provide even better service."

You can discover valuable information by opening the lines of communication between you and your employees or you and your customers. People like to be asked their opinions, especially by someone who listens and cares. (While most companies recoil at the thought of sharing information from a survey with their customers or employees, you can make general statements about your composite results and convey enough information to satisfy their curiosity without compromising yourself or your business in any way.)

Types of Surveys

Surveys are either formal or informal in nature. An example of an informal survey would be asking a group for a show of hands as to whether they would rather see a movie or go to the museum. In this chapter, we will focus on formal surveys. Both formal and informal surveys are used to gather information and measure preferences as a basis for making decisions and taking action.

Formal surveys can be conducted in many different ways, including:

* Face-to-face interviews

* Focus groups

* Written questionnaires

* Telephone interviews.

Assessing Your Needs

Assessing your needs is a process that will help you focus on finding the right solution for the problem you would like to correct. A written survey may or may not be an appropriate way to address problems in your organization. Other possible strategies include interviews, group meetings, focus groups, observation and exit interviews.

What Do We Want to Measure? Why?

Answering these questions as well as the ones that follow is a good way to determine whether your company needs a survey—and whether a survey is the best way to attain the desired information.

- What is it that we really want to know?

- Is information already available that will adequately answer our questions?

- Do the individuals (i.e., employees or customers) have the ability and the willingness to provide the information we ask of them?

- Will knowing the answers to the questions we ask make a difference in the actions we're willing to take on important issues?

Do We Need a Survey?

Planning and conducting a survey can be costly and time-consuming. Yet the information gleaned can be invaluable. Before deciding that a survey is the tool you need, ask yourself:

- Is the need for data important enough to justify the time and money necessary to conduct it?

- Is there a more efficient way to gather the information?

- Do we have the internal and/or external resources necessary to conduct a survey?

- Will we be able to get input from all levels of our organization?

- Will we be willing to act upon the results of the data?

- What will the survey results enable us to do differently that we cannot do presently?

- What short- and long-term gains can we expect?

What Are the Pitfalls?

If the people surveyed have any fear of reprisals or any apprehension whatsoever about how the information will be used, these feelings will affect their responses and render them unreliable. For example: An employee attitude survey conducted by the employer does not carry the assurance of confidentiality that the same survey conducted by an outside organization does. Thus, the two surveys will not bring forth the same information. Results will be skewed in the case of the employer-conducted survey because not all employees will feel they can answer the survey openly and honestly.

Focus groups also have a down-side. Focus group participants may be so pleased to have someone ask their opinions—a rare circumstance for many people—that they may embellish and expound beyond their true findings, thus leading the facilitator to draw erroneous conclusions.

When telephone surveys are conducted, it is imperative that the interviewers be thoroughly trained and that they follow a written script—to the letter. Untrained interviewers or those who fail to take instructions seriously can, by their voice inflection or careless ad-libbing, influence the outcome of the survey. Again, the real danger is that the sponsor of the survey will make decisions based on faulty or inaccurate data.

The possibility of basing decisions for the general population on a biased sample is another risk. A biased sample is a group of people who do not accurately represent the general population. For example: A take-out delicatessen surveyed their customers by giving free samples of a new pasta salad they had developed, then followed the survey with a brief telephone interview. Based on very favorable responses, the delicatessen owner tried marketing the newly developed salad through a chain of grocery stores. It failed. Here are some possible reasons why:

- Customers who were given free samples may have felt obligated to express only positive comments.

- Delicatessen customers like and appreciate the kinds of foods offered at delicatessens as well as the convenience of picking up ready-to-eat foods. Otherwise, they wouldn't be customers.

- Samples handed out in the delicatessen were most likely fresher than the product available through the grocery stores.

- Once in the grocery stores, the product became lost among the hundreds of other items in the refrigerated case that had the advantage of fancier packaging.

Once you ask a question and the respondent knows you know how he/she feels, you have created a new level of expectation. And that expectation is that you will do something with this knowledge. If you ask for and get opinions but fail to act on the new information, your employees' or customers' perceptions of you may turn from favorable—or at least satisfactory—to unfavorable. So think before you ask. You just might get more than you bargained for.

Determining the Kind of Survey to Conduct

Each type of survey discussed below has certain advantages and disadvantages you'll want to consider before deciding which type of survey is best for your needs. Combining one or more surveys can prove advantageous to gathering the most valid insights.

Face-to-Face Interviews

- Face-to-face interviews are an appropriate choice when the information to be gathered requires explanation or is of a highly sensitive nature.

Even though face-to-face interviews are expensive and time-consuming, they are often used to gather information from people who are either experts in their fields or hold upper management positions. The rationale is that these people may be more willing to grant an interview than to complete a survey.

Face-to-face interviews require an experienced interviewer skilled at:

- Putting respondents at ease

- Showing interest in what respondents say while subtly encouraging them to say more

- Being a good listener adept at pursuing a predetermined line of questioning

- Picking up on verbal and non-verbal cues as opportunities to ask spontaneous questions

- Using a friendly, conversational tone of voice with every person.

Focus Groups

Focus groups provide an ideal way to quickly gather information that will help the survey designer develop better questions for a written or telephone interview. A trained facilitator knows how to guide the discussion without actively participating and how to elicit objective data from the group.

While the results of a focus group frequently exhibit the value of simple one-on-one interviews, in and of themselves they are not enough. Focus group responses point the way to asking the right questions in future focus groups, but their scope is too narrow to generalize for larger populations.

Focus group participants are paid to participate, a factor that can distort results if they feel obligated to reply favorably. If participants are brought in from other areas, transportation expenses can cause the overall costs to escalate. Data obtained is qualitative and needs to be supplemented with quantitative measures.

Written Questionnaires

Written questionnaires are used to survey a large or widely dispersed population. This type of survey is less expensive and less labor-intensive than other types of surveys.

Written questionnaires are designed to gather qualitative and quantitative data when all possible responses can be anticipated. Respondents are usually willing to answer one or two open-ended questions that allow them an opportunity to supply information or opinions not yet asked for in the survey.

For example: The one way I would most like to see you improve your service is:_____. By asking the respondent for "the one way," you help him or her to think about and focus on the one thing they would most like to tell you.

Another advantage of the written questionnaire is that it is easy to administer, easy for the respondent to complete at his/her own convenience, and relatively easy to tabulate and analyze with the proper software package.

Telephone Interviews

Telephone interviews are often used by organizations who want to poll many people in a relatively short period of time. The entire job may be put in the hands of a telemarketing service bureau for quick, efficient handling. Questions in telephone interviews need to be kept relatively short. If lengthy answers are needed to provide the information you require, plan to conduct face-to-face interviews instead.

Many people resent being called at home by interviewers, fund-raisers or telemarketers. So even though you may begin with a stratified sample, the ones who agree to talk to you could throw the results into a biased mode.

The telephone interviewers you hire must be capable of maintaining the same enthusiastic, friendly manner in repeated phone calls. Interviewers must be good listeners and skilled in adapting intuitively to a wide range of personalities. They must also be assertive enough to keep people who digress on track.

Planning the Survey

The Importance of Defining Objectives

The purpose of putting your objectives in writing is to help you think through and agree upon what you and others want to accomplish so you'll know when you've finished whether you've met your objectives. Written objectives serve as a checkpoint throughout the development process and can keep you from losing sight of your original intentions.

Your objectives should describe your desired outcomes. What would you like to have happen as a result of the survey? Make a list of all the things you would like to have happen, then consolidate your list into no more than three main objectives. Be sure that everyone involved in developing, administering and analyzing the survey agrees with the objectives and believes they are realistically attainable.

Determine the kind of report you will want before designing the survey. Will you want to include statistical data? If so, what kind?

Your Available Resources

How much money have you budgeted for conducting the survey? Will it be more feasible to handle the complete survey in-house or to hire a competent outside resource? Do you have the expertise to develop, administer and analyze the survey internally and meet your objectives?

Who will do the work? Is their level of expertise up to what you would demand of an outside resource? Do they have the time available? What will have to be let go if you allocate the necessary resources to this effort? Will the payoff warrant the sacrifices?

How much time do you estimate each phase of the survey will take? Will the resources you've selected adhere to this timetable? Will the results still be meaningful and relevant at that time?

The Expertise Required

Each type of survey requires different competencies, skills and experience. If you will be making changes in the way you conduct your business or basing decisions on the results of this survey, it is essential that you assign the work to people with the expertise to gather and report reliable information.

The Importance of Objectivity

One advantage of hiring a competent outside firm is that they can design and analyze the survey with greater objectivity. Objectivity is a necessary component to ensure reliability.

Organizing the Process

There are many ways to gather information for issues addressed in the survey. But the information itself is only one reason for the process; the other reason is to gain buy-in from managers and all other employees. Company-specific surveys, as opposed to standard questionnaires, are much more effective since they can be tailored to the company and the issues that concern it.

Consideration must be made early on regarding the demographic detail necessary. Do you need to know which branch the questionnaires are coming from? Is length of employment important? What else will you want to know?

Try not to raise false expectations in your planning sessions. For example, don't indicate that the survey will result in specific improvements unless you are certain you'll be able to act upon and fund such recommendations. Initial gathering of information for customer surveys should follow this same pattern of planning; actively encourage people from various levels of your organization, especially those who have some contact with customers, to contribute their ideas.

Interviewing sessions, when properly conducted, will provide the information necessary to write your survey questions.

What Should Be the Scope?

If your survey is too long, it may lower your response rate. Ask only what is necessary to achieve your objectives. If your company is interested in feedback on the new software program they have been selling for a year, focus on that one area. If there are other questions you feel compelled to ask, keep them to a minimum.

Who Is Qualified to Conduct the Survey?

There are many valid reasons to use an outside organization skilled in conducting the type of survey you plan to use. You owe it to yourself to interview at least one before making your decision. If you are not using a professional organization to conduct your survey, you need to use individuals in your company who are:

- Assertive but not intimidating to employees
- Respected and responsible
- Ethical
- Personable with excellent interviewing skills (especially for the verbal questioning)
- Goal-oriented
- Highly organized
- Skilled in technical writing and experienced in designing surveys.

What Needs to Be Done?

In chronological order, your survey timetable should consist of:

- Forming a group to pinpoint main objectives
- Deciding on the population to be surveyed

- Conducting preliminary interviews as a basis for writing questions

- Determining the survey method(s) you will use

- Writing and editing your written and/or oral questionnaires

- Selecting your sample group, provided you are not surveying the entire population (See Glossary at the end of this chapter.)

- Selecting your test group and testing the survey instrument

- Holding meetings with those administering the survey to explain the manner in which it is to be conducted, including information about confidentiality and/or anonymity

- Communicating with participants about the survey through a cover letter that explains the purpose of the survey and any special information they should know

- Distributing surveys with complete and clearly written instructions that also restate the purpose

- Having staff available to tabulate questionnaire returns and compile results using an appropriate software package

- Analyzing the data and writing the survey report

- Presenting the survey results to management

- Releasing company-approved survey results to employees or customer survey participants.

When Should the Survey Be Conducted?

Timeliness of issues should always be taken into account. Allow approximately four months minimum to design, conduct and complete your survey. Take into consideration all time constraints, major events, work-loads and any other factors that could adversely affect the outcome of your survey. For example, suppose a hotel sponsoring a medical convention wants participant feedback and suggestions to determine whether they need to implement changes for future conventions. Obviously, they need to conduct their survey soon after the event; therefore, the survey should be drafted before the event takes place.

Additional Considerations

The Anonymity or Confidentiality Question

How important is it that your survey be completely confidential? Your decision to ensure anonymity may be the determining factor as to whether you receive accurate results—or indeed any results—from those not willing to risk identification. Ensuring absolute anonymity has been shown to elicit the most accurate responses, especially when surveying employees. The easiest way for an employee or customer to conceal his/her identity is by giving misleading information regarding personal demographics, such as age, years of service, job status and income level.

Reassure participants in the cover letter and in the instructions to the survey (either written or verbal) that their responses will be kept completely confidential, if this is the case.

Explain the procedure(s) that will be taken to keep the responses or questionnaires confidential. Since demographic questions are frequently altered by survey participants, ask as few demographic questions as possible to achieve your results, and explain to them why this information is needed.

Survey Ethics

Surveys must be written, conducted and reported ethically. You must not mislead anyone about why the survey is being conducted. Explain who is being surveyed, the purpose of the survey, and what will be done with the data. If you promise individual confidentiality, provide it. Unless respondents feel they can trust you, they will not take the questions seriously or answer them honestly.

Ethics come into play at every stage of the survey process. If hiring an outside firm to conduct your survey, ask for assurance of ethical methods and practices. If you are using members of your staff, stress the importance of ethics. Point out that the following practices are unethical and should be avoided at all costs:

- Manipulating numbers or the report for self-serving purposes, or misrepresenting, withholding or downplaying the results to those who have a right to know

- Selecting the population sample intentionally or vicariously for the purpose of influencing results

- Betraying confidences of individual respondents

- Sharing information with other individuals or organizations to win favor, for personal gain or for any other purpose

- Manipulating the truth in any way.

As sponsor of the survey, you have an obligation to design a survey that will elicit objective, unbiased data and to report the information in the same manner.

Developing the Survey

Every survey requires advance preparation based on the objectives and the type of survey you'll be conducting. If someone other than the person(s) designing the survey will be conducting and analyzing the data, include the entire group of people in a planning session so that the survey is designed in the best manner possible to meet the established objectives.

Preparing and Writing the Questions

There are many types of questions from open-ended to forced-choice (see Glossary on page 264). The kinds of questions you use should be determined by the type of information being sought.

Face-to-Face Interviews

Begin the interview with one or two casual questions designed to put the other person at ease. Save any demographic questions until the end of the interview. Prepare two or more versions of open-ended questions for each topic. This will help you gather a greater amount of information without offending or irritating the person being interviewed in case inadequate information is given initially.

Group related questions together and place them in logical sequence so the interview will flow. Establish trust before asking controversial or sensitive questions. Difficult or sensitive questions asked too abruptly could have a negative effect on the rest of the interview.

Interviewing techniques are beyond the scope of this chapter. As stated earlier, face-to-face interviews require the skills of persons trained, experienced and comfortable in this role.

Written Questionnaires

Keep questions short with various forced-choice answers, such as:

- True/false

- Multiple choice

- Yes/no

- Ranking.

Group questions by topic or by the type of responses possible. Place a few easy questions throughout the survey to give the reader a break. But don't ask questions with obvious answers. Ask only enough questions to get the information you need to meet your objectives. Don't leave your most important questions until the end lest people become impatient and begin to rush through the last few. Since demographic questions are usually easy to answer, place them near the end of the survey.

If you include one or more open-ended questions, leave as much space as you feel is necessary for the response. If you don't mind participants writing more, instruct them to use the back of the sheet if necessary. If you want them to use only the space provided, phrase your question accordingly. For example: "Using the space provided, tell the one reason why you most enjoy shopping at XYZ Office Supply Store:_____."

Telephone Interviews

Plan to ask qualifying questions first to determine whether further questions are necessary. For example, a pre-qualifying question for a new pizza delivery service might be, "Do you ever call for pizza delivery?" If the answer is negative, the interviewer could end the survey right there without wasting any more time.

Asking an easy or interesting question first will help put the person being called at ease and may help to arouse interest. Ask the questions in a logical order, keep them simple, and gather the most important information before the person begins to lose interest in the process.

Editing the Questions

Editing with the following criteria in mind will lead to more effective questionnaires:

- *Brevity*—Complex questions should be divided into several shorter ones, and the length of the survey itself should be kept as short as possible.

- *Clarity*—There should be absolutely no confusion or ambiguity about what you are asking. This is why pretesting is essential. It enables you to clarify or eliminate questions that are not being interpreted correctly.

- *Simplicity*—Make as many questions as possible check-off or multiple choice. This not only makes it easier for the survey participants, but for the tabulators as well.

- *Precise instructions*—Just as much care should be taken with instructional wording as with the questions themselves. The initial directions (and all others) should be completely understandable, easily located and set in all caps or bold to set them apart from the survey questions.

Writing and Editing the Cover Letter

A greater reply and return rate usually results when companies take the preliminary step of sending a cover letter. The function of this letter is to set the tone for the survey. It should explain the purpose and provide some basic information about when the person should receive, or be contacted to complete, the survey and when mailed surveys will be returned. It should also include the type of survey you are using, whether it will be confidential, who will be participating and how the results will be used.

The cover letter should be no longer than one page, written in a brief, clear, but friendly manner, and conclude by thanking your employee or customer in advance for his or her anticipated participation.

Have You Given Enough Responses?

Although brevity is key in editing a survey, the options for multiple choice and check-off questions should include all available options a respondent may answer. Make sure categories are not too broad. Here is an example of a bad survey question:

The length of my employment at this bank or one of its affiliate branches is:

a. Less than 6 months

b. At least 6 months but less than 5 years

c. 5 years or more.

A 4-year bank employee may have much more insight than one who has been on the job 6 months; yet these time spans are grouped together. Someone who has worked at the bank 4 years probably will not appreciate being classified with a 6-month employee. Also, a 10- to 15-year bank employee might have insight into current bank management and procedures. However, a bank would not be able to pinpoint responses of 15-year veterans with this categorization. More complete demographic information would result from this choice of responses:

a. = Less than 1 year   d. = 5-10 years

b. = 1-3 years   e. = 10-15 years

c. = 3-5 years   f. = Over 15 years

With this format you would actually use less space. In fact, you would gather more detailed information without lengthening the survey at all.

This very effective question is part of a hospital services survey:

On what date did you most recently use our services?_____

Time of service:

_____ Midnight to 6:00 a.m.

_____ 6:00 a.m. to noon

_____ Noon to 6:00 p.m.

_____ 6:00 p.m. to midnight

The question then asks the respondent to check the box of the service most recently used. Twenty five services are listed. Much information is obtained with little time and complexity involved.

A question from a survey regarding middle-management training proves to be an exercise in confusion, however. Seven categories are listed for each possible training session, but the categories are so ambiguous that a one- to three-line explanation of each is necessary at the bottom of the page. How many times do you think respondents would check the definitions of the categories before guessing or giving up?

Utilizing a Creative Design

The middle-management training survey mentioned above happens to have the look (and length) of an instructional tax booklet. Pages are cramped with large blocks of tiny gray type. Would you want to answer this survey?

Be creative in your questionnaire design. It does pay off. Make your survey stand out with shape, color, graphics or layout, but keep it professional. You want to entice people to look at your survey, but ultimately you want them to read and answer it. Be careful that the overall look compliments the rest of the survey, its tone and objectives. Use a typeface that is easy to read, and space the questions to make them easier to read.

Making Your Survey Work With Your Computer

Attempting to tabulate and cross-tabulate data manually is totally impractical. However, many computer programs are highly effective with projects like survey questionnaires. Consider consulting a software expert if you don't have one.

If you already have a survey program for your computer, design your survey to fit within its limitations. This will make the design, writing and editing of the survey much easier and more efficient. Returns can also be tabulated more readily.

Pretesting Your Survey

Studies show that testing a completed draft of a survey on a group of four to ten people can be very beneficial in helping uncover any problems. The individuals you select for this pretest should not be part of your sample group. But, like your sample group, they should be selected randomly to be sure that the test is effective.

Other Issues

Selecting Your Sample

Whenever you survey 100 percent of a population, you are relieved of the problem of selecting a sample because you are, in fact, surveying everyone. Whenever you plan to survey part of a population, however, it is necessary to select your sample carefully. This involves following statistical methods that are rather complex and beyond the scope of this chapter. You will need to consider the following factors when selecting your sample:

- The expected response rate of the questionnaire

- The precision of the population estimate (For example, there may be times when you do not know the size of the total population you are surveying.)

- The confidence level of your sample (For example, a 95 percent confidence level means that 95 out of 100 times a sample will provide the level of precision desired.)

A representative sample of a target audience allows you to generalize the results and apply them to the entire target audience. By choosing a representative sample, you will save time and money on such items as mailing, data entry and analysis. In selecting a sample, however, you must be certain to make it a random and representative sample. A random sample means that everyone in the target audience has an equal opportunity to be selected to complete your organizational questionnaire. If you choose a sample that is not randomly selected, your choices can greatly influence your findings. Then, when you extrapolate your findings from the sample to the larger population, the size of your error will be greatly magnified.

If you, like many organizations, cannot afford the time, manpower, or financing required to survey the entire target audience you are interested in, focusing your efforts on a sample of the target group will probably be your best choice. Of course, the sample should be chosen entirely at random to prevent skewed results. And, as with any survey audience, your sample population should be informed about how and why they were chosen.

To obtain additional information about selecting a sample or for the formula needed to calculate the minimum sample required, consult "Getting Them Out and Getting Them Back," by Kenneth M. Nowack, in the April 1990 issue of *Training & Development Journal.*

Getting Participant Buy-In

The only way you will get complete cooperation in the development of your survey, a high rate of returns, and the belief from everyone involved that the survey results are valid and useful is if you are able to get participant buy-in. Without the complete cooperation of participants, tabulators and management, it will be impossible for you to meet your objectives.

Therefore, you will want to do everything possible to obtain participant buy-in. One of the most effective ways to do that is to involve others from all management levels in the process from the very beginning. If you're conducting a customer survey, then you'll want a variety of customers to contribute to the content of the survey. In either case, communicate this fact to all employees or customers. Once they know that their peers were active in helping to develop the questionnaire, they will be more likely to buy into it. Throughout the survey process, remind them that this survey is in no way a one-(wo)man show.

When conducting an employee survey, have employees contribute suggestions anonymously by mail or through a suggestion box. Ask customers to mail in their suggestions, or interview a small number of them by telephone to get their input and suggestions about the survey. Participants will be flattered if you ask them to share their opinions. Doing so will also lend credibility to your commitment to the survey process.

Increasing Your Response Rate

Typical response rates for surveys mailed to customers or clients range from 33 to 65 percent, depending on the strength of the relationship between the survey sponsor and the person asked to respond. Other factors that affect the response rate are whether letters precede the survey and whether incentives for responding are included with the survey.

Analyzing the Results

Tabulating the data and analyzing the results should be assigned to a professional fully attuned to the purpose and objectives of the survey or to people within your organization who will in no way benefit from the results. The latter situation could be difficult to assess.

For example, on a customer survey questioning the need for an extended product line, it would be inappropriate to have the new product manager organizing tabulations. No one who might recognize employees' or co-workers' handwriting should have access to the surveys either. In the case of open-ended questions on employee surveys, the people responsible for compiling final results must be able to summarize and group responses without changing the meaning of the responses.

Finally, the person on the team analyzing the results must be very familiar with the inner workings of the organization and possess outstanding analytical abilities and good reporting skills.

Compiling the Final Report

The final report should follow the format of a formal research report and should include:

*   An executive summary

*   Introduction and/or purpose

*   Method

*   Scope

*   Presentation of data

*   Discussion

*   Summary

*   Conclusion

*   Exact copy of the research instrument

*   Statistical findings, graphs, tables and charts (optional).

Developing an Action Plan

Did the survey meet your objectives? Was the survey conducted in such a manner that you believe in the validity of the findings? Now that you know the results, what actions must be taken? How will you gain acceptance for these decisions? Has the survey provided you with valuable information? Continually refer to the findings and analysis as you develop your action plans, and even later as you implement the plan. A good survey should serve as a benchmark for future measurements and as a blueprint for decisions as long as the information remains current and valid.

Communicating the Results and Your Plan of Action

For both employee and customer surveys, it is recommended that you let the participants in the survey know something about the survey results and your plan of action. You do not have to reveal exact data or confidential information. Customers should receive personalized letters, if possible.

Employee survey results may be released through a newsletter, an announcement or an all-employee meeting. For example, "Our survey results on the addition of a cafeteria surprised us: 75 percent of the employees indicated they had no interest in such a facility. So our plans for this will be set aside. Since 80 percent of you with small children indicated you would use a day care center, we are now studying ways to address that issue. Expect more information within 90 days." (Remember: When reporting results of a survey, do not suggest your willingness to act on issues unless you intend to carry through.)

A Powerful Business Tool

A professionally developed survey is a powerful business tool. Customers and employees recognize this as one of the few ways they can voice their ideas and opinions to the companies they work for, or with whom they do business. Progressive businesses have learned that it is profitable to listen and act upon reasonable requests and suggestions of their customers. Valuable insights and suggestions come from surveys that would not surface otherwise. By purposefully utilizing employee input, your company can successfully maintain a satisfied, productive and efficient work force.

If you would like more information on surveys, consult the following articles: "Customer-Service Perceptions and Reality" by Wendy S. Becker and Richard S. Wellins (*Training & Development Journal,* March 1990) and "Need Marketing Information? Tips for Successful Surveys" by Richard P. Gorman of Association Management, Inc., Washington, D.C. (*Sales and Marketing Executive Report,* sample issue.)

Glossary

Bias—Anything in a survey that intentionally or inadvertently influences the results.

Forced-choice questions—Those questions in which the respondent must choose from the answers provided, such as a multiple choice question.

Open-ended questions—Beginnings of sentences that require more than a one word answer. The respondent completes the question in a random sample in his or her own words to express true opinions or feelings.

Population—All the people who could provide the information you want to collect.

Sample—The group of people you select to actually survey. There may be 5,000 people in the company divided between six divisions and ten departments. Your sample includes people from each department in every division.

Stratified random sampling—A group randomly selected from pre-selected groups, such as the departments within a company.

Sub-population—Groups within the population that you need to include in your survey, e.g., all departments within a company.

CHAPTER 12

PREPARING YOUR COMPANY'S FIRST ANNUAL REPORT

Although producing an annual report is not required by law, many companies are spending considerable time and money on their annual reports. While publicly held companies must satisfy the needs of their stockholders through an annual report, small privately held companies may be better off allocating their resources to other endeavors, such as building their business.

This chapter is written for those individuals involved in producing their company's annual report. If this is your first time, or you've run into problems in the past, you'll find this chapter helpful. In it you will learn how to:

- Determine whether you have the in-house capability to produce your own annual report

- Ensure that the proper information is included in your report

- Select a designer or design firm, if you elect to use one

- Develop an effective schedule for the production process.

Consider the Benefits

Annual reports, which frequently rival the best periodicals in graphics, photography and text, are no longer simply about business—they are business. An annual report can benefit your business by:

- Establishing and promoting a sound corporate image

- Attracting new investors

- Bringing goals and objectives into focus

- Tracking company goals and objectives

- Explaining company actions and spending decisions

- Recording company history.

Get Involved—Stay Involved

Annual reports are frequently produced by a team of graphic artists, photographers, designers, writers, editors and printers who are rarely full-time employees of the company. Your challenge is to produce a professional annual report without losing control of the finished product. You must get involved and stay involved to make certain that your company's vision is the one communicated in the final report.

Writing and producing an annual report is not a job for amateurs. Although you will want to listen to and consider all suggestions offered by the professionals you hire to assist you, you are in the best position to provide the theme that will unite the final product. You are also responsible for ensuring that the annual report accurately reflects your company. Whether you use a full-time writer and a design firm or produce the document internally, you must be involved in the production process from start to finish. Only in this way can you achieve a high-quality report that correctly represents your company.

Getting Started

Because the writing process is a team effort and cannot be performed effectively by only one person, you owe it to yourself to hand-pick a group of key people. Together, you will explore ideas and make many important decisions before actually writing the report. The entire team, including writers, designers, photographers and printers, must be involved from the very beginning. No team member's work will be complete until the report has been printed and distributed. The following guidelines will help you and your team set attainable goals and will make your initial planning efforts more productive.

• Appoint a committee to oversee the production process. Enlist the help of employees or corporate board members who have report experience.

• Establish your objectives for the report.

• Determine the amount of time and resources that your staff can dedicate to the project.

• Insist that designers, editors, and writers attend regularly scheduled meetings so that you can check their progress and discuss any problems. Stay in touch with each team member—never assume that the job will get done.

• Establish your report budget. Keep in mind that annual report costs can range from $20,000 to $150,000 or more. Regardless of the budget, spend carefully to make certain you stay within your limits.

• Read other companies' annual reports for theme and text ideas (available in most libraries). Also, subscribe to newsletters that critique annual reports; they will keep you informed about the latest controversies and design concepts. (Consult page 274 for additional information.)

- Appoint two or three committee members to interview design firms, writers and photographers. After the interviews are completed, have these members present their findings to the entire committee. Let the final selection be a team effort.

- Determine who will oversee the production process, the schedule and the budget. Include a representative from the company's accounting firm to monitor the report budget.

- Select several people, including committee members and others who are not on the committee, to read, edit and approve the final draft These readers will bring a fresh viewpoint to the document and may catch errors and oversights that frequent readers of the document missed.

After you have carefully considered all of the above guidelines and have decided to produce your annual report, it is imperative that you recognize the complexity of the task you are undertaking. You will need capable, supportive personnel and outside resources to do a good job.

The Production Process

Most annual reports are based on calendar-year operations. Major production activities begin in mid-December; mailings are usually scheduled for mid-March. In some companies, active work on the annual report begins as early as September; however, unless you are planning to significantly change your company's existing image, all you need to do in early fall is begin the process of selecting your design firm.

The release date for annual reports usually precedes the annual meeting as determined by the corporation's by-laws, requirements of the exchange on which the corporation's stock is listed, or SEC regulations. However, your preparations will begin long before the release date. The first step in the production process is to develop a production schedule. This is because a production schedule:

- Permits you and others to check the report's progress at any time

- Condenses all the details that will be reflected in the final product while maintaining the "big picture"

- Prevents oversights and omissions of important steps

- Helps you meet interim deadlines and the final delivery date.

The best way to prepare your timetable is to work backward from the mailing date and estimate the time required for each step. Be prepared to revise the schedule once or twice during the production process. Also, consider incorporating periodic one- to two-day "cushions" to allow for unscheduled revisions and unexpected problems.

Keep a detailed log of procedures as work progresses. Enter the date of each item's completion in an "Actual Date" column. Use a "Contact" column to note who is responsible for the items and a "Reference" column for thoughts and follow-up ideas. You will find this reference column especially useful when preparing next

year's report. A more detailed schedule should list
timetables and specifications for ordering paper, writing
newspaper releases and accompanying photographers on
their shoots. A sample schedule for smaller corporations
and a more detailed schedule for larger corporations are
included at the end of this chapter.

Hiring Your Marketing or Design Firm

The right marketing or design firm will create graphic elements and oversee the photography, layout, typesetting and printing of your annual report. They can
help you find an editor as well as a photographer skilled
in industrial photography. They can accompany you on
photo shoots to determine if the lighting and angles are
right for creating the look you want. And they can coor-
dinate all the production phases, order your paper stock,
and provide professional proofreaders for the first prints.

Professional designers can also save you money by
subcontracting with other professionals; they can coordi-
nate all the production details and, if you communicate
your wishes to them, can ensure the unity of the finished
project. Be sure to begin your search as soon as possible; the best design firms commit to projects early.

The ability to work in concert with your design firm
is not a commodity that can be easily measured. However, several criteria can help you in your search for the
right designer or design group. Begin by interviewing at
least three design groups. If you don't know where to
find candidates, check the Yellow Pages under "marketing." Also, ask other business owners for their recommendations, or review their annual reports to learn about
the quality of local agencies. Keep in mind that

although proximity to a design firm is a definite advantage, quality should be your first priority. Hiring a firm that is close but incapable of producing quality work would be a poor decision.

When interviewing potential designers/design firms, use the following interview methods to help you make a wise choice:

- Contact several firms by telephone and ask them some key questions regarding your needs and their experience. After you have spoken to several, choose the three that impressed you the most and set up interviews with them. These three interviewees should have experience writing annual reports and should provide samples of their work at the interview. If they do not include annual reports in the samples they bring, select another firm. This is the one project on which you can't afford to take a chance on an unknown. Look for and hire a designer who is experienced in financial reporting.

- Look closely at the work the firm has done for others. Apply the same criteria to their samples that you will apply to your own finished report: Do the design and text complement each other? How effectively does the design convey the company's image? Does the design appeal to you? Ask questions about which aspects of the job were under their direction.

- Once you have narrowed your search to those firms whose work you like, ask for a complete written bid that includes a breakdown for design, photographer and photographs, editing and proofreading, typesetting and professional printing. Be candid regarding the dollar range you have budgeted for design. Being evasive or arbitrary may cause them to overbid the job, which will slow the production   process or—worse yet—lose you the opportunity to work with a top-notch firm. Also, remember that a great portion of the budget will be dedicated to printing, especially if you plan to use color photographs and/or expensive foils, die-cuts and embosses.

• Ask for references and then check thoroughly with the names provided. Did the firm meet their deadlines? Did they complete the project within budget? Was the working relationship satisfactory? Was the quality up to their expectations?

• After you select a design firm and receive several design ideas from them, you may get a sinking feeling that you made a poor choice. Because this is a possibility, include kill fees as part of your design agreement. Don't expect the other party to suggest them or be responsible for them. Kill fees, which are specified in the contract before the project begins, will allow you to dissolve your relationship fairly if the need arises. Usually the kill fee is 5 to 20 percent of the total design estimate. The kill fee option must be accompanied by your assurance that none of their work will be used in the finished product.

Because photographs are frequently used in annual reports, it is also important to include use fees in your agreement. Use fees usually refer to ownership of photographs. New copyright laws enable photographers to retain rights, meaning that they can charge you according to the number of times you use the photographs. Under this arrangement, the photographer owns all photographs you do not use in your current project and also has future rights to the photographs that you do use. If the contract states that fees include only one-time rights, you will be charged if you choose to use the annual report photos in another publication.

You must negotiate use fees before you sign anything. Ask your attorney to see that your contract reads "all-rights" and gives you ownership of all photos and negatives at the end of the project. Not all photographers retain rights. These photographers work for a fee, and the pictures and negatives are yours when the project is complete.

Finally, it is extremely important that you find a competent, reliable and trustworthy designer that you like, both personally and professionally. Because the text and the design must work together, the writer, designer and project manager should view their relationship as a three-way partnership.

Once you have chosen your firm, involve the designers in all meetings and actively seek their advice on the image you want to present this year. Early involvement will allow time for them to help develop your theme, generate enthusiasm for the project and create graphic elements that complement your report. Also, establish periodic meeting dates well in advance to keep all the communication lines open and your project on schedule.

One note of caution: Some designers pay little attention to the needs of their clients because they believe their clients know very little about design and marketing. A good designer will listen to the client and then enhance the client's ideas in a way that is visually and graphically pleasing. Beware of designers who create designs to be entered into design competitions to win awards for themselves. Unless their choice of design is one that reflects your company accurately, don't succumb to pressure to "be more creative." It's your company, your image, and your money—you want the annual report to reflect that. Be clear about what you want. Recognize the difference between a designer's ego-driven recommendation and a helpful, expert suggestion and you will avoid buying a design that pleases the designer rather than your company.

Choosing a Theme

Currently, many professionals are debating the merits of using themes in annual reports. Some designers and producers believe that conveying good information is what is truly important and an overall theme for the report is simply unnecessary. Although a theme is optional, there are some very good reasons for having one. A theme can:

- Help convey your message more succinctly on both verbal and subliminal levels

- Build and enhance your corporate image

- Help unite the text and the overall graphic design

- Provide interesting reading (which helps ensure that the report is read).

You may already have a theme in mind; perhaps you know that you want your shareholders to perceive your company as one that works hard to protect the environment. You could develop that image in text by discussing your new employee ride-share program and writing about the "plant-a-tree" campaign that your company launched in a new industrial development. Including photographs that support the theme and printing the annual report on recycled paper would further promote an "environmentally friendly" image.

Hasbro, Inc. played on the theme of "Time flies when you're having fun" for its 1992 Annual Report. Pictures of Hasbro classics—including Tinkertoy, G.I. Joe and Easy-Bake Oven—appear throughout the report, as they were way-back-when and as they are today. Complementing this nostalgic look back are numerous photographs of Hasbro's best-selling products and trend-setters of 1992. The body of the report focuses on the company's growth and acquisitions, showing readers the tremendous strides they have made in the last year.

In their 1992 Annual Report, Johnson & Johnson set out to show their stockholders "the nature and impor-tance of our business outside the U.S." Most people—stockholders included—don't realize that almost half of Johnson & Johnson's sales are international, according to CEO Ralph S. Larsen. Shaped by the theme "Growth in World Markets," the report takes the reader around the globe to various markets reliant on Johnson & Johnson products and highlights those products, many of which are unavailable in the U.S.

If you don't already have a theme in mind, here's how to generate ideas that will help you develop an appropriate theme:

- List all of the major business events that occurred in the past year

- Categorize the items on the list. Some suggested headings include product development, physical growth, expanded services and new markets

- Check past press releases

- Ask for contributions from other key individuals.

One or more theme ideas should emerge from your list. If you added several new positions, bought additional property and expanded your production space, your theme might be "Positioned for the Future" or "Expanding Technologies to Meet Tomorrow's Demands." You may decide, once you've made this list, to keep it updated for next year's report.

Your design firm can also be an invaluable resource when choosing your theme. The designers are familiar with trends and current styles that may be just what you are seeking and can offer valuable input on how to visually and graphically develop your theme.

Writing the Report

After you have completed the background work, hired a design firm and chosen a theme, it is time to begin the writing process. Provide the primary writer with plenty of background on the company and its product(s) or service(s). You may want to work with the writer to develop an outline so that the writer's actual writing time is well-spent. Also, be sure to check his or her progress several times throughout the writing process. It is important to give the outside writer a contact person within the company who is readily accessible to answer questions and is well-informed about the goals and objectives you have set. Whether you are working with an outside writer or have decided to write the report in-house, you should begin by outlining your report and sketching out what you will include.

Outline Your Report

Each annual report, whether from a small company, a conglomerate or a non-profit organization, has several common elements.

"OK, the question before the board is this: What genre should we choose for this year's report to the stockholders? Fiction or Non-Fiction?"

A Company Profile

This reflects the corporate culture and includes a brief history of the company, its goals, objectives, markets, products/services and mission. This section could be written by the company president, a vice president or a long-term employee.

A Letter from the President

This letter serves as an overview or synopsis of the report. Often in the past, another person wrote this letter for the officer to sign; however, today's CEOs want to present a friendlier, more approachable image, so many are writing their own letters.

The president's letter is the place to explain if the year was not very profitable, if the company restructured to meet future demands or any other difficult news. Although your investors may not enjoy hearing this news, they expect an explanation from the president.

Some companies have built their entire annual report around bad news, as Gerber Products did in 1987 and General Motors did in 1992. In the Gerber report, the first paragraph of the president's letter read, "As you will note by the theme of this Annual Report, 'Reaching Tomorrow Today,' fiscal year 1987 was a year of building for your company. Although sales increased nine percent to $917,320,000, net earnings from continuing operations declined 16 percent to $317,147,000. This decline in net earnings was, in many ways, a result of the building program."

The body of the text in Gerber's Annual Report was broken down by products with subheads "Today" and "Tomorrow." In this way, Gerber reinforced the idea that the investments made today would bring returns tomorrow. Likewise, GM printed its '92 annual report in black and white to reflect a year of losses—the largest losses experienced in the company's history—and cut-backs.

A Financial Report

The most popular way to present the company financial report is to print sections from the company's Form 10-K with accompanying notes. You may also opt to print a "highlights" section, which is simply a compilation of your quarterly reports with brief explanations. Suggested writers for this section are the president or chief financial officer.

A Signed and Dated Report of Certified Public Accountant

This section, which should be approximately two paragraphs long, is required by the SEC (Securities and Exchange Commission) to ensure that all your financial information has been verified. An Independent CPA or Auditor must write and sign this section.

The Report Body

The report body may include sections about various new products/services, market segments, physical growth, acquisitions, restructuring information, international operations, or even, as in the case of Waste Management's 1992 Annual Report, a special section of "essays" addressing the timely topic of the environment. Waste Management interviewed six children from around the world about their concerns, concerns ranging from air pollution to "keeping the sea clean." Each child's essay appears at the top of a page, followed by ways Waste Management is working to improve the environment.

Another good example can be seen in Merck's 1992 Annual Report. This pharmaceutical manufacturer had a vested interest in addressing one of the hottest topics of the election year, health-care reform. Under a section titled just that, Merck asserts that "at this time the 'managed competition' model, in our view, comes closest to promising solutions to our health-care crisis." Under this model, pharmaceutical manufacturers like Merck wouldn't have to worry about limiting their research and development programs, programs which greatly affect their bottom line.

As you are writing, use vocabulary that is specific to your industry. You can gain this information from press releases, brochures, and other like materials. Do not, however, use jargon; and never assume that others are familiar with key words and phrases you hear around the office every day. For example, just because everyone in the office furniture industry knows the meaning of "ergonomically designed systems" doesn't mean your audience does. If you cannot substitute synonyms, include a glossary of terms in the back of the report.

Although these sections are not mandatory, you may also want to include financial comparisons with previous year(s), information on corporate structure, and biographies of key personnel.

The Report Design

The overall report design should reflect your company's products and values. Take, for example, Adobe's 1992 Annual Report. The overall look is very design-oriented, with vibrant colors, different typefaces in varying sizes and even abstract photos. In Adobe's case, the approach works because it positions them as a cutting-edge graphic arts software company—just the image they wish to portray. The same look applied to a bank, however, would send a different message, one of instability and risk. That's why, throughout the conceptual stage, you need to work closely with your design firm and check carefully to see that they are carrying out your specifications and meeting your design preferences.

Because visuals often tell the story more quickly and effectively than words, use graphs and charts to convey good news more dramatically. With today's computers, graphs can be made 3-dimensional, and many companies are taking advantage of this; however, be sure that your graphs fit the information and that they are visually and technically correct. For example, use a pie chart when numbers add up to 100 percent, a line graph to show trends, and a bar graph to compare and contrast data.

Don't feel compelled to use traditional-looking graphs and charts, however. Toys 'R' Us showed they could break out of the mold in their playful 1992-1993 Annual Report. They incorporated their mascot Geoffrey Giraffe into several bar graphs throughout. For example, in a graph titled "10 Year Growth of a 100 Share Investment in Toys 'R' Us Stock," Geoffrey's neck grows longer as stocks increase in value.

The cover of your report is also very important; it will be your readers' first impression of your report and will set the tone for what's inside. The cover design should be treated as part of the entire report. It should invite the reader to pick up the report and should support your company's message. As your cover design develops, remember that glitz is not always best. Some of the most attractive annual reports sport simple one-color glossy covers. Most report covers include the name of the company and the year, and some also include a title, often the theme of the report. Your company's image, theme, product and/or service will help determine the design.

Finally, use columns, white space, call-outs (second-color type that can stand by itself or design elements that seem to flow from page to page) and subheads rather than titles throughout the report.

Assign Additional Information Providers

Employees, vice-presidents, engineers, salespeople and department heads may be able to provide information that will enrich and supplement the information you receive from other sources. Ask these people to present their information in written, narrative form. Someone on your production team should write an introduction to each section so that your information providers will know what is expected from them. Give them a copy of this outline along with a summary of your theme and apprise them of your schedule and deadlines. Clarify that you require their expertise in content only; the primary writer/editor will incorporate their information into the final text. Finally, have faith in your contributors—most will live up to your expectations.

All submissions from the additional information providers should be typed double-spaced and should be given to the primary writer before he or she begins any work.

Review the Report

Periodically check with the people you've requested information from throughout the writing process. This will allow you to assess progress and provide feedback.

Once you have received all of the information needed for the report, review it to make sure that all the necessary data has been included and is correct. Any additions or deletions should be made before you submit the sections to the primary writer. It is a good idea to have several people from both inside and outside the company review the information for clarity and content. Does it make sense to them? Are the outside readers' questions answered in the text? Is the tone appropriate throughout?

Focus on the Audience

Be sure to give all of your writers some information about those who will be reading the report, such as investors, employees, stockbrokers and potential investors. What do these people want to know? Make sure that the writers keep these people in mind and write as if they were answering all the questions that their readers may ask about the last business year. Tell them to write clearly and concisely without oversimplifying, to be considerate without patronizing.

Send the Report to a Professional Editor

Whether you write your report in-house or use the services of an outside writer, this is an important step. The editor you hire should be well-versed in financial reporting. A local English teacher or newspaper stringer is not the right person for this important project. Many marketing design firms have professional editors on staff or on call; they can help you find the right person. If your design firm does recommend an editor, ask for his or her references and check them carefully before you commit to using the editor's services. After you have chosen an editor, meet with him or her well in advance of your actual need for services to schedule your project. Also, be sure to get a firm price or a per-page figure so you know what the entire job will cost. Allow enough time in your production schedule for at least two edits and three proofreadings.

Take Your Report to a Professional Printer

Although in-house printing is adequate for everyday reports and letters, you will want to have your annual report printed by a professional printer. If you are working with a reputable design firm, this shouldn't be a worry; they will have established a good working relationship with a quality printer and will interact with the printer directly on your project. If you are producing your report in-house, however, you will need to seek out a qualified printer. The printer you choose should possess 4- to 6-color printing capabilities (the means to produce color graphs and illustrations). Also look for a printer with a reputation for precise registration and proper color balance. A substandard printing job will make even the best writing and design work look bad.

Remember, if you go with a design firm, you're paying them to oversee the printing of the report. The firm will know how to communicate the requirements of the job to the printer and what to look for when checking proofs. Although you will certainly want to look at the proofs, leave the actual proofing to the experts.

Before You Begin

Keep these additional hints in mind as you produce your annual report:

- The annual report can serve many purposes, only one of which is projecting your company's image. The report is not a public relations "fluff piece." Keep it factual with every element supporting the theme.

- Once you decide to produce an annual report, you should publish one every year. It is not good public relations strategy to produce a report only when the news is good and then to send your 10-K to the SEC following less profitable years.

- Make sure your text is honest—even if it was not your best year. Address the issues, state the facts in the president's letter and move on.

- Focus on the year at hand. An annual report is not the place to discuss old news, old products and old business.

The Rewards

As you and your team prepare to write your company's annual report, commit to staying involved throughout the entire production process. Set aside individual agendas and work together to effectively convey your ideas and goals for the finished product. Plan on the production process taking more time than initially anticipated, especially if this is your first annual report. Anticipating delays and rewrites will keep you from becoming discouraged or frantic during the process.

If you plan carefully, select an experienced and reputable design firm and stay involved throughout the process, you will be rewarded with an impressive report that accurately reflects your company's image and long-range goals and honestly apprises your readers of the information they need to know.

For more information regarding the newsletter that critiques annual reports, contact: Sid Cato Communications, P.O. Box 738, Waukesha, WI 53187-0738, (414) 549-3200.

The following pages contain sample worksheets to help you stay on schedule when producing your annual report.

Sample Schedule for Producing an Annual Report

The information provided here is to serve as a guide in developing your own schedule. Delete or add tasks, as required to tailor this worksheet to your specific needs and requirements.

Schedule Date	Actual Date	Action	Reference	Contact
Sept. 15		First item, meet with key people to communicate your decision to produce an annual report. Solicit their ideas. Give them an overview of the work involved and the contribution you'll need from each of them. Get them to buy-in to the process and allocate time in their schedules to complete assigned tasks.		
Sept. 30		Meet with and request basic material from all department heads; gather past news releases, in-house documents and meeting minutes for important information. Develop a work schedule, assigning due dates to tasks. Set up interviews with prospective visual communication firms.		
Oct. 1		Collect and categorize all information and write a rough draft of text. Determine project budget and number of reports to be printed. Determine special printing specifications. Solicit proposal(s) from the most competent visual communication firm(s).		

Schedule Date	Actual Date	Action	Reference	Contact
Nov. 1		Select and contract a visual communication firm and schedule an initial meeting to supply content information, rough draft of text, discuss theme ideas and review important due dates.		
Dec. 1		Design/writing firm submits revised text and design mockups for review and sets up photo shoot.		
Jan. 1		Revised test is distributed to department heads for verification and proofing. Check with board of directors, executive officers and members of management committees for correct spellings of names and titles for the director's and officer's page. Approval is given on a general theme and design layout.		
Jan. 15		Text is returned to visual communication firm with corrections and recommendations.		
Feb. 1		Request final version of financials be sent to CPA firm; advise CPA firm of certification deadlines.		
Feb. 10		Information for graphs and statistical charts along with final version of financials are submitted to visual communication firm.		

Schedule Date	Actual Date	Action	Reference	Contact
Feb. 20		Review of complete piece with final draft incorporated with all pre-approved photos, artwork and financials. Final proofing of piece by department heads and a proofreader. Final approval is given to the visual communication firm .		
Mar. 1		Visual communication firm oversees production and coordinates the final printing of report.		
Mar. 15		Receive and distribute annual report. Prepare press releases and send to newspapers.		

FINAL THOUGHTS . . .

While there is no absolute formula for making a success of your own business, there are certain criteria for ensuring your success. Many of these have already been discussed in the previous chapters; but here are a few final thoughts that come to mind based on my own business experience and my consulting work with other business executives.

Strategies to Maximize Your Potential

Commitment

Operating your own business requires tremendous commitment. Sometimes you'll be the only one who believes in what you're doing. That's when you must be dedicated enough—committed enough to perservere—until others share the vision you've had all along.

Adaptability

Many who start businesses are technicians—good at what they do. They find a need and they fill it; and the business grows. But there comes a time in the life of a business when being a technician doesn't "work" any more. As the business grows, it needs someone who can lead—plan—develop strategies and make decisions which will affect financial outcomes. Business owners who fail to negotiate the choppy waters at this critical juncture curtail their own opportunities for growth and, in fact, may not survive. You must continually adapt to change.

Self Development

Self development is the key and must be part of your success strategy. Attend seminars. Listen to tapes. Go to trade shows. Read trade publications and books. Set goals for yourself—challenging goals. What are the important areas to develop? Start with these:

- Ability to be an effective communicator so you can express your thoughts and ideas.

- Ability to plan, organize and set priorities. This is the only way you'll accomplish all that you must to stay ahead of your competition.

- Ability to be sensitive to the needs of others—to pick up on subtleties and respond appropriately. Be willing to go the extra mile without thought of personal gain.

- Ability to analyze situations, data and trends. You must be able to spot relationships and separate the relevant from the irrelevant in order to solve problems.

- Ability to make judgments. Every day you'll be required to weigh the options, assess potential outcomes, make decisions and accept the risks that go with those decisions. The more your business grows the faster they'll come. You must become adept at making good decisions and living with the consequences.

The Numbers

Another key to growth is running your business by the numbers. Know what the important ratios are for your business then track your expenses and the ratios religiously. No matter how good the bottom line looks, continually seek ways to increase your margins and decrease expenses. But don't be short-sighted. Compromising quality or service would not be in the best interest of your company.

Personnel

Hire good people—the best people you can afford and the best you can find. Treat them well. Help them develop their potential. Bring them into the decision-making process and show them what's in it for them. Give them incentive to do their best, then reward them for outstanding performance. That's the key to having a stable workforce; that's the key to meeting your goals. You can't do it by yourself, so hire good people.

Ethical Issues

Ethical issues and issues of integrity surface often in business. Customers, employees, suppliers will put you to the test and at times catch you off guard. The only advice I can give here is play by the rules. Then and only then can you expect your people to do the same. Then and only then will you command the respect of your clients, co-workers, competitors and counterparts in other industries.

Community Involvement

As your business grows you will find increasing opportunities for community involvement. Business leaders are expected to contribute to their communities, after all, they're the ones who get things done. Payoffs come slowly and intermittently, so don't get involved for the rewards. In time, the people you meet, the good that you do, the community you build will enhance your image and the image of your company and generally make you a better person. And all this is good, as long as you don't let your commitment to community get ahead of commitment to your business.

Balance

One of the greatest challenges for business owners is achieving and maintaining balance in their lives. Jim Rohn in his Nightengale-Conant tape series, *The Art of Exceptional Living*, states "Regardless of what you're working on in life there's only about a half a dozen things that make 80% of the difference." I believe there's only about a half dozen things in life that make 80% of the difference. And as important as my business is to me, it's only one part of my life—just one of a half dozen others. Balance and perspective—key ingredients of a successful life.

To Your Success,

About High-Impact Marketing Services

High-Impact Marketing Services, now in its seventh year of business, helps companies and individuals market themselves more effectively. We serve primarily business owners and marketing executives whose goal is to become No. 1 in their fields and who are willing to commit the resources needed to reach their goals. We enjoy a high level of repeat business from our clients, who are most often in businesses where image and perceptions are important.

High-Impact clients include major furniture, chemical and pharmaceutical manufacturers, financial consultants, financial institutions, CPA firms, software developers and many for-profit organizations in diverse fields, such as real estate, water purification, packaged goods marketing and health care.

High-Impact provides consulting services, conducts customer/client satisfaction surveys, develops strategic marketing plans, and designs corporate identity packages. Additional services include writing, designing and producing brochures, capability statements, direct mail campaigns, promotional newsletters and custom sales presentation materials.

Send for Your Free Subscription Today

For a complimentary subscription to *High-Impact Communication Line,* our quarterly newsletter, mail or fax your request, with your business card, to: High-Impact Marketing Services, 2505 East Paris Road S.E., Suite 130, Grand Rapids, Michigan 49546. Fax number: (616) 949-0204.